Disc Dogs:
The Complete Guide

By World Champions
Peter Bloeme & Jeff Perry

Hyperflite, Inc.
Atlanta, Georgia

Bryan Speed

This edition is dedicated to the next generation of dog lovers and disc doggers: Sydney and Wesley Bloeme, Sarah Miller, Benjamin, Galen, Lindy, and Piper Perry.

Cover photograph of Timmie Dohn's dog Shenzi by Sven Van Driessche. Title page photograph of Chuck Middleton's Hank by Bryan Speed.

Every effort has been made to trace the copyright holders and models of the photographs used in this book. Should there be any mistakes or omissions in this respect, the publisher apologizes and shall be pleased to make the appropriate acknowledgments in any future printing.

TRADEMARKS: Frisbee is a registered trademark of Wham-O, Inc. Hyperflite and K-10 are registered trademarks of Hyperflite, Inc. Competition Standard, Disc Dogs! The Complete Guide, Disc Dog Training DVD, FrostBite disc, FrostBite Pup disc, Jawz disc, Jawz Pup disc, K-10 Pup disc, Midnight Sun disc, PAWS, SofFlite disc, SofFlite Pup disc, UV disc, and PAWS Freestyle Scoring System are trademarks of Hyperflite, Inc. Skyhoundz is a registered trademark of PRB & Associates, Inc.

ISBN 978-0-9817237-0-9 | First Edition/First Printing June 2008

Library of Congress Control Number: 2008926008

To order additional copies of this book, contact the publisher: Hyperflite, Inc., www.hyperflite.com. Printed in Hong Kong.

Peter Bloeme

"Gilbert" taking off for a long distance throw in Tokyo, Japan.

Pairs Freestyle! Twice as much fun for your dog.

Sven Van Driessche

No need for a "leg up" for "Maty," a three-legged canine at the 2006 Hyperflite Skyhoundz World Championship.

Contents

Peter Bloeme

Two-Time World Champion "Nick" jumping for his favorite toy!

Peter Bloeme

Chuck Hensley and "Rascal!"

This edition would not have been possible without the assistance of a dedicated cadre of disc dog enthusiasts. In particular we appreciate greatly the assistance of the following people without whom publication of this book would not have been possible: *Dennis Alexander, Jeremy Angel, John & Shannon Bilheimer, Adrian & Tracy Custer, Todd Duncan, Danny Eggleston, Ron Ellis, Bob Evans, Gerell Evans, George Freeman, Martha Gill, Ralph Grieblinger, Chuck Hensley, Jeff Hoot, Ed Jakubowski, Shaun Johnson, Troy Kerstetter, Kendall Lemley, Long Photography, Inc., Ray Lowman, Patrick Major, Walt Mancini, Susan Markham, Chuck Middleton, Mike & Kathy Miller, Jay Moldow, Frank Montgomery, Mark Muir, Theresa Musi, Darren Neff, Nancy Noel, Hiromi Orihara, Lynne Ouchida, Jackie Parkin, Angie Perry, Greg & Marjorie Perry, Dan "Stork" Roddick, Yukihiro Sekiguchi, Len Silvester, Bryan Speed, Jeff & Angie Stanaway, Alex Stein, Nyle "Swanee" Swainston, David Turrentine, Sven Van Driessche, Hilde Van Durme, Phil Van Tee, Christopher Vitale, Bill Watters, Paul West, Dolores Willis, and Peter Wouters.*

Disc Surfer.

I first met Peter Bloeme while competing at a regional-level competition in the mid-1980's with my animal shelter-adoptee *Gilbert*. At the regional, despite our best efforts, *Gilbert* and I finished fourth. Naturally, I wanted to improve my performance in future years so, after the contest, I approached Bloeme, then a national judge, for some tips and advice. Bloeme had won the World Championship with his dog *Whirlin' Wizard* a few years earlier.

We spent about 20 minutes chatting after the contest — going over, in detail, what I needed to do to improve. Bloeme suggested that I reorganize my routine, develop some innovative new tricks, drop tricks that had a low margin for success, and consider using music that would get the crowd energized. Finally, he reminded me to have fun when I was competing so as to avoid taking the fun out of the experience for my canine. In essence, after talking with Bloeme, it was obvious that a complete restructuring of my routine was necessary if I wanted to take it to the next level.

Jeff Perry and "Toulouse"...yes, even Miniature Poodles enjoy disc play.

Peter Bloeme

Peter Bloeme

1989 World Champion "Gilbert" at the
Olympic Stadium in Berlin, Germany.

Jeff Perry and "K.D." performing a butterfly "backflip."

During the off-season I swallowed the bitter pill, so to speak, and started over from scratch. The following year, *Gilbert* and I won the Southeast Regional thereby qualifying to compete in the World Finals. A few years later, in 1989, we won the World Championship in Dallas, Texas. After the competition, Bloeme approached me about becoming a judge and member of the celebrity touring team that promoted the competition series on behalf of the sponsor.

Being on the celebrity touring team meant that I would have to make numerous media appearances as well as perform at international promotional events in Canada, Europe, Japan, and Mexico, among other locales. I was flattered but not sure I was quite ready to give up competing. Bloeme knew that rescuing shelter dogs was a cause near and dear to my heart and he reminded

me that being a celebrity spokesperson would be a great way of getting that important message out to the masses. I was sold.

Not long after I began judging and promoting the national contest series,

"Gilbert" was always popular with NFL cheerleaders.

Bloeme asked me to assist him with a special project; namely, editing and contributing to what would become the seminal book about canine disc sports — *Frisbee Dogs: How to Raise, Train and Compete.*

Frisbee Dogs was a runaway hit. Tens of thousands of copies were sold, with versions in English as well as in Japanese. *Frisbee Dogs* was published in two editions, with the second edition released in 1994.

Since 1994 the sport has evolved, matured and grown exponentially. When Bloeme published *Frisbee Dogs*, there was only one company making canine discs and the design was nearly as old as the pie tin on which it was based! At a pivotal moment in the history of canine disc sports, Bloeme and I (along with Greg Perry) established Hyperflite because of our belief that existing flying disc manufacturers had

"Gilbert's" trademark was his spectacular "backflips."

neglected to offer innovations that kept pace with the evolving abilities of the modern canine athlete.

Although Bloeme and I planned for many years to release a third edition of *Frisbee Dogs*, the rapid evolution of canine disc sports convinced us that any such effort would be quickly outdated. Now, at last, *Disc Dogs! The Complete Guide* is ready. *Disc Dogs!* features detailed training information, color photos and numerous features that make it a worthy successor to the original.

So curl up in a comfortable chair with your faithful friend at your feet and enjoy *Disc Dogs!*

— Jeff Perry
1989 World Champion
Co-Founder, Hyperflite, Inc.

Perry judging for Fuji Television in Tokyo, Japan.

GRAVY

In 1994, on one of our early disc dog sojourns to the island nation of Japan, we were privileged to help introduce canine disc sports to the Japanese populace via Fuji Television's heavily promoted "Year of the Dog" celebration. On one of our free days, we rode the ever-efficient Japanese subway system to the Shibuya station in Tokyo, to make a pilgrimage of sorts.

Only a few steps outside of one of the entrances to the Shibuya station, we found ourselves at the base of a large bronze statue of a canine of legendary faithfulness. The inspiring and true story of "Hachiko," is one that touches the heart of anyone who has every shared a special bond with a canine.

"Chu-ken Hachiko" (translation — the faithful dog "Hachiko") and his human companion, Isaburo Uyeno, a professor at a nearby University, came to Tokyo in 1924. Each day, Uyeno, accompanied by "Hachiko," walked to the Shibuya train station where Uyeno departed for work. "Hachiko" would then wait patiently at the station until Mr. Uyeno returned from his job at the University.

In 1925, Uyeno became ill and died suddenly while working at the University. Even though "Hachiko" was only 2 years of age at the time of Uyeno's passing, the bond of affection between them would last for the rest of "Hachiko's" life. Venturing home only occasionally, "Hachiko" would remain at the station for days at a time waiting for his friend to return from the University. He kept his vigil for the next 11 years, finally passing away at the spot where he last saw his best friend alive. Over the years, many were inspired by "Hachiko's" faithfulness. In 1934 a statute was erected to honor this special dog and the lesson that his loyalty and love taught to those who knew of his devotion.

Mindful of the lesson of "Hachiko," we began contemplating a way to remind disc doggers of the unconditional love and faithfulness expressed by virtually all canines toward their human caretakers. In the end, we decided that a Latin phrase summed up these feelings most succinctly. The phrase, "Fidelis Caninus Amiculus," which means "faithful canine friend" was added to all Hyperflite award medals beginning with the 2007 canine disc season.

— *Peter Bloeme and Jeff Perry*

"Sassy" doing a brilliant "chest vault" off of Ping Latvong.

Foreword

In memory of Irv Lander, the founding father of canine disc sports, the original foreword from *Frisbee Dogs: How to Raise Train and Compete*, appears below:

It's very entertaining to see dogs soaring through the air to catch flying discs, but Frisbee dogs don't just miraculously develop overnight. Training even the most adaptable breeds, like Australian Shepherds, Border Collies and Labrador Retrievers, requires dedication and patience to achieve gratifying results.

When Peter Bloeme asked me to write a foreword for this book, I was flattered. As co-founder and Executive Director of the Ashley Whippet Invitational, along with my 10-year stint as Vice President and member of the Board of Directors of the Los Angeles Society for the Prevention of Cruelty to Animals, I have seen many newspaper articles and books written about Frisbee play and dog training. Many writers, in an attempt to be cute or funny, have not taken the subject seriously. Bloeme has worked long and hard to achieve personal

Irv Lander and Peter Bloeme during the "CBS Youth Invitational" television show in Atlanta, Georgia.

Peter Bloeme, Irv Lander, and Alex Stein during a rehearsal for a Dallas Cowboy halftime show.

success and professional stature by being a pioneer in the sport, a world champion, a professional performer, a national judge, a world-class dog trainer and now Director of the Friskies Canine Frisbee disc Championships. He takes disc sports seriously, which is why you'll find the material in this book authoritative and sincere.

In any event, I received the invitation to set the tone of this truly excellent and comprehensive work on the care and training of a Frisbee dog with much enthusiasm. Bloeme sets high standards of perfection for himself and others.

Is the book timely? Does it fill a need? Emphatically, yes! The national interest in acquiring and training a dog to be adept at

Alex Stein & "Ashley Whippet," Irv Lander, and Peter Bloeme & "Wizard."

Irv Lander teaching "First Daughter" Amy Carter how to throw a disc to "Ashley Whippet" on the White House lawn.

catching a Frisbee disc is at an all-time high thanks to the exploits of high-flying canines on television and in the print media.

Individuals who now own an untrained dog, or who plan to acquire one, will benefit greatly from this book. Bloeme shares with the reader his many experiences as a gifted athlete and the methods he used to train the undefeated 1984 World Champion "Whirlin' Wizard," his beloved Border Collie. And Bloeme does it in a down-to-earth, narrative style that, while factual and logical, makes for fascinating reading. Although, it may be true that every expert is not necessarily a good teacher, Bloeme is the real thing. He gives you practical step-by-step guidance, not theory, with his uncanny knack for making complex things seem simple.

Reading this book in manuscript form, I became even more aware of Bloeme's greatest asset: perseverance. Without perseverance in the pursuit of learning and excellence, one will not achieve success to the desired degree. The key is there for you

in this book, but you must not be impatient or give up along the way.

Many people have told me they were inspired to procure and train a Frisbee dog after seeing Bloeme perform with "Wizard" on television or in a stadium. Now they, and you, can intimately share his unique repertoire of tricks by owning this book and by reading and re-reading it thoroughly.

If you're serious about raising and training a Frisbee dog, and becoming a skilled thrower as well, this book by Peter Bloeme is a must. Like Bloeme it is World Class in every respect.

— Irv Lander (1917-1998)
Executive Director
Ashley Whippet Invitational

I first met Irv Lander when I was 15 years old in Las Vegas where I competed in Wham-O's Junior National Frisbee Championships, a human disc-tossing championship. I had earned my invitation through wins at the city, state and

"Wizard" racing down the field for a long distance throw from Peter Bloeme.

regional level. Lander was the Director of the championship.

I finished third overall and first in distance out of more than one and a half million junior competitors from all over the United States. After the tournament, I wrote Lander a letter thanking

"Casey" doing some required reading.

him for running the contest in a professional and smooth manner. In return, I received an unexpected and memorable reply. He wrote:

> "…Although you did not achieve your goal this time, you were far and away the most spectacular Frisbee performer in the history of our National Junior Frisbee Championships.
>
> "Surely there will be many additional honors that your skills and dedication will earn for you in the future. I am certain that your name will be prominent in adult Frisbee competition for years to come…"

Since then, Lander went on to become a great influence in my personal and professional life, and working with him was always a pleasure and an honor.

— **Peter Bloeme**
1984 World Champion
Co-Founder Hyperflite, Inc.

Jeff Perry & "Gilbert," Alex Stein & "Ashley Jr."
and Peter Bloeme & "Wizard" in Berlin, Germany.

Why yes! I'll be happy to "jawtograph" your disc.

Nearly 20 years ago, with the publication of *Frisbee Dogs: How to Raise Train and Compete*, we attempted to answer the question, *Why teach your canine to play with a flying disc?* Today, just as then, there are as many answers to that query as there are participants in canine disc sports. One chord rings true in nearly every enthusiast's experience with disc dog sports. Simply put — people engage in canine disc play because their dogs absolutely love it.

Canine disc play is not only fun for dogs, it can also help to provide challenges, both mental and physical, that will help a canine feel that it is living a full and productive life. The shared activity of canine disc play will create a special bond of friendship and mutual respect that will help both canine and human relate better to one another.

Over the years, canine disc aficionados have shared with us countless stories of depressed and destructive canines whose lives were turned around solely because of their involvement in disc sports. These bored and direction-less canines suddenly had a regular activity in their lives that stimulated them mentally and exhausted them physically. At the end of the day, dogs that used to bounce off the walls would sleep contentedly at their masters' feet.

Authors Peter Bloeme and Jeff Perry with the Skyhoundz World Championship Cup.

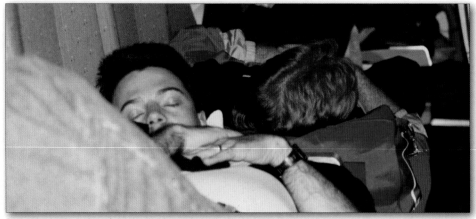

Promoting the sport throughout the world is a tough job, but someone has to do it.

People with hectic schedules have discovered that ten minutes of disc play, in the backyard or at a nearby park, is more fun and better exercise for a canine than an hour-long walk.

Competitions abound for disc dog lovers who wish to show their stuff on the playing field. The Hyperflite Skyhoundz Series, the largest canine disc competition series in the world, has seen a dramatic increase in participation at its events in recent years. Soon the Hyperflite Skyhoundz Series will feature more than 200 competitions worldwide.

Also benefiting from the popularity of canine disc sports are animal shelters and rescue organizations. It's no secret that shelter canines, in addition to making wonderful family pets, make fabulous disc dogs as well. Many active disc doggers seek out shelter animals that most folks would regard as unadoptable by virtue of their destructive tendencies and nervous energy. In fact, nearly half of the canines that have won World Championship titles in competition have been mixed-breed canines, many of which were adopted from shelters and rescue organizations by their proud owners. Unlike some other canine activities, disc dog competitions are open to all dogs regardless of pedigree or skill level.

Almost everyone loves to watch the grace and fluidity of a well-trained canine athlete being put through its paces by an experienced human teammate. Just ask anyone who has ever watched a top canine disc team perform at a National Football League halftime. Disc dogs steal the show every time.

Peter Bloeme and Jeff Perry in Puerto Rico training their disc pigeons.

Facts — Facts are kernels of information that may, or may not, relate to disc dogs, but will be of interest to lovers of the canine species.

Gravy for Disc Dog Aficionados — These heart-warming, real-life stories are a great reminder of why canine disc play is such a meaningful part of the lives of enthusiasts.

Web Links — In this information-centric world, enthusiasts want current information and they want it fast! The Link icon directs you to online resources that contain the most up-to-date information available including, but not limited to, competition schedules, disc dog products, disc dog club listings, etc.

Pro Tips — Pro Tips, gleaned from some of the best trainers and competitors in the sport, offer gems of wisdom that will benefit even the most experienced disc doggers.

And then there is the disc dog way of life. In ever increasing quantities, large and vibrant sub-communities of *rabid* disc dog participants are springing up in nearly every American state and most countries as well. These social groups, called disc dog clubs, bring together dog lovers who have discovered that disc dogging is not merely great exercise, but a way of life as well. They eat, drink, breathe, and dream disc dogs.

Why teach your canine to play with a flying disc? We say — why not!

ABOUT THIS BOOK

Disc Dogs! The Complete Guide is designed to offer something for everyone — and for good reason. Disc dog sports by their nature offer all people, and all canines, a fun and healthful activity that enthusiasts can pursue casually or very competitively.

Throughout the book we have included a number of special features that are set apart from the regular text by icons as shown above.

Book chapters in *Disc Dogs!* are organized to help you find the subject matter that is most relevant to the activity in which you are participating. For example, if you are already an accomplished disc thrower, you may choose to skip the Throwing chapter and head straight for Disc Dogs! Advanced. If you want to surf the chapters, then by all means, feel free to do so. However, be advised that you may miss some beautiful color photos of disc dogs in action.

Disc Dogs! is written for all levels of experience. Although many people choose to compete, the vast majority of canine disc enthusiasts limit their play to a backyard or local park. Consequently, many readers will choose to ignore the chapter on competition. We recognize that just as some people are intrigued and excited by the idea of competing in a disc dog competition, others are intimidated or perhaps even fearful of performing in front of crowds and more experienced competitors. We have been

Authors Peter Bloeme and Jeff Perry..."then."

staging disc dog competitions for more than 20 years and never — not even once — has a competitor been booed or jeered at for having a bad day on the playing field. To the contrary, competitors and spectators alike understand that the dogs are out there to have fun and whether or not we humans take home a trophy for the mantle, just isn't relevant to our pets. Unlike most forms of competition, there is camaraderie and a general atmosphere of helpfulness at disc dog competitions. Hyperflite Skyhoundz competitions over the years have featured disabled canines, wheelchair-equipped throwers, senior citizens, youngsters, men and women, hearing and vision impaired canines and/or throwers, and just about every level of skill and enthusiasm that you can imagine. Inclusiveness is the word that describes the Hyperflite Skyhoundz World Championship Series. You owe it to your canine to, at least once, compete for fun in a Hyperflite Skyhoundz

competition. It just might change your life! Hyperflite Skyhoundz canine disc competitions are free and ubiquitous. *And not only that,* as Gilligan might say, *they're everywhere.*

LINK   For a schedule of Hyperflite Skyhoundz Competitions, please visit: http://skyhoundz.com

Throughout *Disc Dogs!,* for simplicity, we employ male pronouns in reference to canines in general and canine training specifically.

Finally, because *Disc Dogs!* is a collaborative effort by two World Champions, the pronoun *we* is used to describe our collective opinion or impression on a particular point. When helpful, our personal experiences are highlighted in such a manner as to be readily apparent to the reader.

Now, let's begin our journey through the fascinating and exciting world of canine disc sports.

— **Peter Bloeme and Jeff Perry**

FACT

Canine whiskers called vibrissae, found on the muzzles of our four-legged friends, are actually capable of sensing minute changes in airflow. If only these same vibrissae could be designed into canine discs. Imagine a disc that could adjust in flight to compensate for our less-than-perfect throws!

GRAVY

Adopting shelter and rescue animals isn't just a corporate slogan at Hyperflite…it's part of our DNA. Every owner and staff member of our company has at least one shelter or rescue animal. So, when my kids began pestering me for a dog of their own, following the passing of our family dog, I knew it was time to pay a visit to the Atlanta Humane Society. Without telling anyone, a few days before Christmas, I ventured out to begin the quest for a new "family member."

Little did I know what a daunting experience it would prove to be. There were hundreds of eager and excited dogs housed in their large warehouse building. After several hours of looking, I picked "Roxie," a sweet-natured Labrador mix. "Roxie" had been tied up in a backyard and completely ignored for all of her eight months of life.

I couldn't take her home right away because "Roxie" would need to be spayed before she could leave the shelter.

The Monday following the holiday, I surprised the kids with the news that we could go to the shelter and look at dogs. I would, of course, have the final say as to the dog we adopted. They were ecstatic. I told them we could look at puppies, but we were not going to adopt one of them because, it was the older, less adoptable dogs, that needed homes the most.

So, off we went, my ten-year-old son Wesley and seven-year-old daughter Sydney, eager and excited. We started out playing with the kittens and puppies. When it was time to go into the big "scary" room full of dogs, Wesley bowed out because of all the noise and commotion. So, it was Sydney and I who walked up and down the rows of kennels looking for a dog to adopt.

Sydney patiently looked at every dog in every kennel. Finally, we came to "Roxie's" kennel. "Roxie" got up and came over to the door. Sydney stopped, looked up in my eyes, and said, "Daddy, what about this one?" I was shocked that, without any prompting, out of the many dogs we had just seen, that we had both chosen the same dog… or maybe, it was the dog who chose us. "Sydney," I said, tearing up at the serendipity of the moment, "I think you made an excellent choice — we'll adopt her."

— Peter Bloeme, 1984 World Champion

PRO TIP

Shelter Dogs — Shelter and rescue animals make great disc dogs. Although most people think that Border Collies, Australian Shepherds, Labradors and Golden Retrievers make the best disc dogs, nothing could be further from the truth. A loved dog, makes a great disc dog and very few canines are loved more than adopted shelter and rescue canines.

— Jeff Perry, 1989 World Champion

Now let's see...where was that photographer?

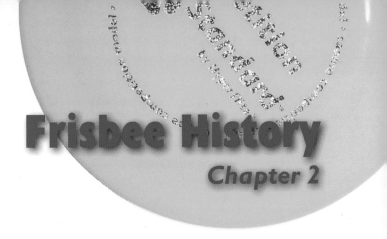

Frisbee History

Chapter 2

Most people with disc dogs are led to the sport by their canines and are usually unaware of the early history of the flying disc. Even those who gravitate to canine disc sports from other disciplines usually are quite oblivious to the pedigree of our beloved plastic platter. However, the history of the disc is quite interesting and certainly worth knowing.

In 1871, a man named William Russell Frisbie settled in Bridgeport, Connecticut and took over the management of a new bakery. Soon after, he bought it outright and renamed it *The Frisbie Pie Company*. At its peak it turned out more than 80,000 pies per day!

Of the Frisbee brand flying disc, Gay Talese of the *New York Times* wrote on August 11, 1957:

> "Possibly the name is used in recognition of the Frisbie Baking Company of Bridgeport, Connecticut, which after World War II had a clientele notoriously famous for not returning tin pie plates.
>
> 'Somebody discovered a pie-plate-pitching game and it was found that our tin plates were excellent for scaling (throwing),' a company official said. 'During that fad we lost about 5,000 tin pie plates.'"

Two weeks later, on August 25, 1957, the *Times* published the following letter:

> "...It is common knowledge in New Haven that Frisbie has been played at Yale for over a century...at Yale, birthplace of the sport, Frisbie is a heritage — a whole way of life."

Credit for the development of the modern plastic product can be given to Walter Fred Morrison, whose father invented the sealed-beam auto headlight. In 1947 Morrison carved the first flying disc from a block of tenite (an early plastic). He soon found that tenite was too brittle, so in 1948 he used a plastic that could be molded.

According to Dr. Stancil E.D. Johnson in his book, *Frisbee*, "This original Morrison's Flyin' Saucer was his Arcuate Vane Model, named for the six topside (flight plate) curved spoilers (vanes)…Curiously, the spoilers were on backward; that is, they would theoretically work only for a counterclockwise spin." That disc was the predecessor of today's Frisbee discs.

In late 1955, Wham-O Manufacturing Company (hereafter simply referred to as Wham-O) founders, Rich Knerr and A.K. Spud Melin (who started their company in a garage where they produced sling shots), saw the Pluto Platter (Morrison's revised Arcuate Vane) and liked the product so much that they purchased the rights to manufacture and sell it.

On January 13, 1957 the first Pluto Platter rolled off the Wham-O production line. In 1958 the *Frisbie Pie Company* went out of business — signaling the end of one era and the beginning of another.

Dr. Johnson also wrote in his book *Frisbee*:

"On a trip to the campuses of the Ivy League, Knerr first heard the term 'frisbie.' Harvard students said they'd tossed pie tins around for years and called it frisbieing. Knerr liked the terms frisbie and frisbieing, so he borrowed them. Having no idea of the historical origins, he spelled the saucer Frisbee, phonetically correct, but one vowel away from the Frisbie Pie Company."

And in the May 1975 edition of *Oui Magazine*, James R. Petersen wrote:

"To avoid legal trouble with the Frisbie Pie Company, Fred Morrison changed the ie to ee and patented the Frisbee Flying Disk [sic]. It was a cosmic example of name it and claim it. Like Kleenex, like Xerox,

Jeff Perry

No one could have guessed that there would be a disc dog World Championship when the flying disc was invented.

Frisbee became the noun for all varieties of the product. Unlike Kleenex, like Xerox, Frisbee also became a verb and a way of life."

On May 26, 1959, Wham-O was granted a registered trademark on the word Frisbee. It is trademark number 679,186 for *"Toy flying saucers for toss games."* Called everything from disc, to disk, to sport disc, to flying disc, to flying saucer, there has never been a more widely accepted name for this product than the original term Frisbee (Frisbee disc by Wham-O), which has been in use for nearly 50 years.

The meaning behind the word Frisbee transcends the flying disc. It is, and has always been both sport and a way of life. Since its first use as a pie tin, this toy became a fad, turned into a game, then a sport, and took off in popularity. Disc play has gained respectability. Today it's taught and played in many schools and universities. There is now a World Flying Disc Federation based in Sweden

Are you ready to play?

with 26 member nations as well as a number of contests, mail order businesses, web retailers, and publications devoted to this world-class sport.

GRAVY

At the 2006 Hyperflite Skyhoundz World Canine Disc Championship, 75 of the top canines in the world qualified to compete for the title of World Champion. Merely qualifying for the World Championship is a huge accomplishment for even the most gifted of canines. But one of the canines, "Maty," an animal shelter mutt belonging to Lynne Ouchida and Troy Kerstetter of Bend, Oregon, gave a "leg up," to the other competitors right from the start. That's because "Maty" was missing one of her hind legs.

Despite her situation, "'Maty' fetches with the best of them," claims a proud Kerstetter. "'Maty' doesn't think that she is any different than the other dogs and we don't treat her any differently," Ouchida, adds. "Maty" was a big hit at the 2006 Worlds and turned in a sensational performance catching every toss made by Kerstetter, including one out-of-bounds throw! "Maty's" stellar effort allowed the pair to finish in seventh place in a field of 24 of the world's elite canines in the Expert Class of the Sport Division.

— ***Troy Kerstetter (and Lynne Ouchida), 2006 World Finalist, Sport Division***

Super "back vault!"

Close up view of the "Fastback Frisbee disc" by Wham-O.

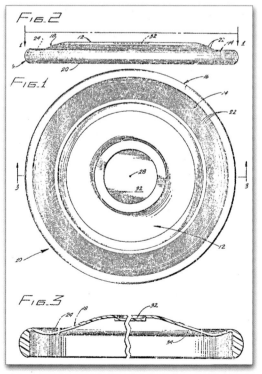

FIG.2

FIG.1

FIG.3

The figure at left is a Wham-O patent drawing of the *Fastback Frisbee disc*. This text is from the patent description.

"*Over the past decade, toys resembling inverted platters or saucers have enjoyed great popularity as recreational items for use in throwing games and contests. In the usual embodiment the toy is made of a plastic material in a circular configuration with a rim portion located at its periphery, the rim portion being relatively thick in comparison to the remaining portions of the implement. In its normal inverted platter orientation, the rim curves downwardly from the toy body giving the implement a shape which approximates that of an airfoil when viewed in elevation. Such a toy has been marketed for the period indicated above by the assignee of the present application under the trademark Frisbee.*"

*Bulldogs, with their strong jaws, need
ultra-tough discs like the Hyperflite "Jawz disc."*

Canine Disc History
Chapter 3

No one actually knows the identity of the first person to throw a disc to a canine, but the credit for first popularizing this activity must go to Alex Stein, owner and trainer of the legendary three-time world canine disc champion, *Ashley Whippet*. Besides being his registered name, *Ashley* actually was a Whippet; a breed that looks like a small Greyhound — sleek, smooth, short-haired, athletic and very fast.

Ashley was born in Oxford, Ohio on October 2, 1971. Stein received him as a gift and took him everywhere. He soon discovered that he had no ordinary run-of-the-mill dog! *Ashley* would chase, leap, spin in the air and catch just about any disc thrown (which at the time were large diameter Super Pro Frisbee discs).

Stein had the intuition that *Ashley* could make it in show business, so he boldly moved from Cleveland, Ohio to Hollywood, California; the land of opportunity for the unusual.

Alex Stein clowning it up for the camera with "Ashley Whippet." Notice the large disc "Ashley" had to catch.

Peter Bloeme

Alex Stein and "Ashley Whippet."

feet, spun in the air and caught flying discs. They answered, *"You have a dog that can run how fast, jump how high and catch what?"* Although it proved difficult to find an agent who would take him seriously, rather than give up, Stein approached Wham-O, the maker of Frisbee brand discs.

At first, Wham-O showed little interest, so Stein dreamed up a way to attract their attention. He wanted to demonstrate that Ashley was attention-grabbing, exciting, newsworthy and entertaining. Fortunately for the sport, both Stein and *Ashley* had great courage and determination.

So in August of 1974, Stein smuggled *Ashley* into Dodger Stadium during a nationally televised baseball game. Between the seventh and eighth innings, the duo borrowed the outfield from the major leaguers and performed for eight minutes before

When he called the various talent agencies, he told them he had a dog that ran 35 miles-per-hour, jumped nine

Walt Mancini

Alex Stein performing with "Ashley Whippet."

Peter Bloeme

Alex Stein serving up another story...

Why *Ashley* was so talented no one knows. Whippets, in general, are not renowned disc dogs. Still, we have never seen a dog more beautiful and graceful, or as high a leaper as *Ashley* was.

After an action packed life of entertaining millions and popularizing an exciting activity for owners and their dogs, *Ashley Whippet* passed away on March 11, 1985 at the age of 14.

In his lifetime, *Ashley* set the standards for the sport. Yet he was just the beginning. People often ask us who is, or was, the greatest disc dog. We can't compare *Ashley* or other great dogs of the past with the champions of today because of the sport's rapid growth and evolution. New tricks, rules and training methods have all added variables that make comparisons impossible.

Alex Stein toured for a number of years with *Ashley's* pups, *Ashley Jr.*, *Ashley III*, and *Lady Ashley* as a member

Stein was arrested. Their debut almost turned catastrophic when, during the arrest, *Ashley* disappeared.

Irv Lander, then Director of the International Frisbee Association, happened to be at the game and bailed Stein out of jail. For three days, both men were sick with worry at the thought that *Ashley* might be lost forever. Fortunately, a boy who had seen the performance found *Ashley* roaming the stadium parking lot, took him home and cared for him until his parents could get in touch with Stein.

The crowd at Dodger Stadium loved the impromptu show and their exploits brought the pair national publicity.

After that memorable baseball game, Stein and *Ashley* became legendary performing at Super Bowl XII, The Tonight Show, Merv Griffin, Late Night with David Letterman and even at the White House for Amy Carter. Then, when competition began for canines, *Ashley* ran away with three world titles.

Walt Mancini

"Hyper Hank" watches while "Ashley Whippet" flies to make a catch.

of the Ashley Whippet Invitational Celebrity Touring Team. Several years ago he settled down, got married, and had a daughter. Recently he moved his family to Stowe, Vermont and opened *Edelweiss*, a Deli/Convenience Store (2251 Mountain Rd, Stowe, Vermont 05672). If you're in the area, be sure to stop by. The food is excellent and there is no better storyteller of the days of old than Stein who is always willing to serve up another one.

Another popular team deserving credit for making the sport what it is today, is Eldon McIntire and his Australian Shepherd, *Hyper Hank*. They rank high in the annals of canine disc history, and few dogs were as aptly named. *Hyper Hank* perfectly complemented *Ashley Whippet*. *Ashley* was small, sleek and mellow; *Hank* was large, hairy and excitable, hence the name Hyper. He would run through a wall to catch a disc. McIntire and *Hyper*

Hank frequently toured with Stein and *Ashley*. Their many historic canine disc performances together included performances at the Super Bowl and at the White House.

Although the dogs themselves frequently get the accolades (and rightfully so), we would not be where we are today without the incredible dedication, drive, energy and support of Irv Lander, who was always a dog lover.

After seeing these great dogs perform, Lander felt that an opportunity existed to provide a sponsor with an attention-grabbing event and dog lovers with an exciting sport. A competition would serve many purposes. For a sponsor, it would provide a unique promotional opportunity. For dog owners, it would physically challenge them to learn new throws, tricks and techniques. For dogs it would provide great exercise and an opportunity to compete as a team with their owners.

"First Daughter" Amy Carter playing with "Hyper Hank" on the White House lawn.

"Ashley Jr." skying for a disc.

Peter Bloeme

Lander, who had worked closely for many years with the Society for the Prevention of Cruelty to Animals (SPCA) in Los Angeles, felt that an additional side benefit of the sport of canine disc would be to encourage people to adopt pets from shelters. And what better way to take that message to the masses than with canine disc competitions?

The first canine disc contest of note was held in 1974 at California State University at Fullerton, with radio station KFI and Wham-O as co-sponsors. It was called the *First Annual Fearless Fido Frisbee Fetching Fracas*. What a classic name! More than 100 canines entered. Alex Stein and *Ashley Whippet* were considered ringers (too professional) and were not allowed to compete. Two of *Ashley's* good friends, Eldon McIntire with *Hyper Hank* and Ken Gorman with *Schatzie*, took the top honors.

The next major canine disc event was a series of demonstrations sponsored by Wham-O at the Rose Bowl during the 1974 World Frisbee Championships. Following that, the competition series that existed at the time became known as Catch & Fetch contests sponsored by Kal Kan.

In the early days, the contest was typically held in conjunction with the World Frisbee Championships at the Rose Bowl. Later, with the support of a corporate sponsor, Lander was able to redesign the event so that it could stand on its own.

From 1978-1988, Gaines Dog Foods maintained the sponsorship of the world championships for disc-catching athletes. In 1989 there was no national sponsor. From 1990-2000, various Nestlé dog food brands, including ALPO and Come 'N Get It continued sponsorship of the national series in the U.S., which was composed of numerous local competitions, six regional championships and a world finals. Regardless of the sponsorship arrangement, competitors typically referred to the event as the Ashley Whippet Invitational or AWI.

In 1990, to honor Lander's efforts, we proposed the idea of a trophy cup

Jeff Perry and Peter Bloeme presenting the "Lander Cup" to Irv Lander.

to honor the man who meant so much to the sport. We designed the cup and had it made by an established trophy shop in Atlanta. The members of the AWI Celebrity Touring Team (Peter Bloeme, Eldon McIntire, Jeff Perry, and Alex Stein) shared the costs of what would become the *Lander Cup* and presented it to Lander at the World Finals Awards Banquet.

Lander made many sacrifices to establish the sport. He worked on a shoestring budget the first few years, staying in unsavory motels while on the road, and spent a great deal of his personal savings in order to ensure the contest's success.

Sadly, in 1998, Irv Lander passed away. Much loved by his loyal staff and indeed, by the entire disc dog community, Lander was undoubtedly,

the right man, at the right time, for a very important job. Any movement of significance needs a father and Lander was not only the father of disc dog sports, but a father figure for many of us, during the important formative years of canine disc sports.

A New Canine Disc Era Dawns

With Lander's passing, and owing to the advent of the internet, canine disc sports began a period of rapid change. A number of fledgling contest series emerged and offered more competitive choices for canine disc enthusiasts. Disc dog clubs were beginning to stage their own unaffiliated contests. Reaching out to large numbers of people, affordably, via the worldwide web was within the grasp of anyone with a mind to stage a disc dog contest. The Ashley Whippet Invitational series was no longer the only game in town.

A few years prior to his passing, Lander and the authors began to discuss a succession plan for the Ashley Whippet Invitational series.

In fact, on July 19, 1994, Lander wrote Bloeme:

> "As a reward for your years of devoted service to this company and [for] maintaining the high standards established, you will have exclusive first right of refusal to acquire this company and its assets, at a price to be determined as mutually acceptable, no later than early 1998, but possibly sooner."

We engaged in numerous discussions and exchanges about the future of the AWI series and we saw *eye-to-eye* on the core philosophy that a national series should be composed of free local events, regionals and a world championship and that the events should be as inclusive as possible. Lander knew from our discussions that, if necessary, we were prepared to continue the contest series, (as he did in 1989) without a major sponsor, at our own expense. Our sponsor was made aware that Lander intended to transfer control of the AWI series to Skyhoundz in the near future. Unfortunately, Lander passed suddenly before we were able to complete a formal transfer of the series. Just prior to Lander's death, Steve Lander, one of Lander's sons, decided that he wanted to take over management of the contest despite Lander's previous commitment to Skyhoundz.

GRAVY

When Alex Stein was living in Sierra Madre in the late seventies, he bred "Ashley" to "Sophie," and they had their first litter. I lived nearby and after a few visits to Stein's place, I took a liking to one of the puppies. When they were weaned, Stein traded "Walter" to me for a Frisbie Pie tin of mine that he really wanted.

As "Walter" grew up, of course I attempted to train him as a Frisbee dog, but that didn't go exceptionally well. He was enthusiastic, but never really aggressive about leaping for the disc like his dad. I would take "Walter" with me almost everywhere I went. As he got bigger, folks who saw us would often mistake him for "Ashley Whippet."

They'd say, "Hey, that's 'Ashley Whippet,' the great Frisbee dog, isn't it?"

I'd have to say, "No, actually it's not 'Ashley Whippet,' but it's his son, Walter."

Then they'd usually come back with, "Wow, I'll bet he's a great Frisbee player too, huh?"

My typical reply was, "Well, are you familiar with Mickey Mantel's son, Billy?"

They'd say, "Uh... no, I don't think I have heard of him..."

And I'd say, "Exactly..."

Not that I didn't love him just the same. I guess no puppy could have lived up to that particular dad.

— *Dan "Stork" Roddick, PhD*
Former Director of the International Frisbee Association (IFA)

Up to that point, Lander's son Steve hadn't been active in the management or conduct of the competition series and was also very involved with a full-time law practice in Northern California. It would prove difficult for him to devote the time required to address the needs of the sponsor while managing his active law practice. The Series sponsor, ALPO, hired Bloeme to serve as a consultant, on their behalf, during Steve's first full year (1999) to make sure things ran smoothly.

The following year (2000), the contest sponsor decided not to sponsor the AWI series with Steve Lander at the helm. They did, however, agree to sponsor a Skyhoundz competition series that would have, essentially, the same elements as the original AWI series, namely, a series of local and regional events culminating in a world championship. That year, the first Skyhoundz World Championship was held in New York City's Central Park. The World

Championship was a great success with incredible media coverage. We were optimistic about future sponsorship. During the off-season Nestlé S.A. (owner of the ALPO brand) began the process of acquiring the Purina Dog Food Company. We wondered if this development would impact their involvement with the Skyhoundz series. We didn't have to wonder for very long as we received notification that the sponsorship contract would not be renewed. With the contest series facing a sponsor-less year for the second time in its history, maximum efforts were made to secure a sponsor that would continue the series. The financial commitment was substantial and, in the end, despite some interest from companies that were not a good fit (an electronic shock collar company, a soft drink company and a beer company, to name a few!), we opted to go it alone. In so doing, we resolved never to be faced with the dilemma of a sponsor-less year again.

Peter Bloeme getting ready to make a long distance throw to "Ashley Whippet" at a race track demonstration.

Sponsorship, an essential element of the national contest series was, from the beginning, an uncontrollable variable. Each year, despite Bloeme's, Lander's, McIntire's, and Perry's best efforts, we never knew for sure whether the sponsor would renew until the last minute…when it was too late to secure a new sponsor for the following year.

Earlier in 2001, we first considered the possibility that Hyperflite — our fledgling canine disc company — could assume sponsorship of the Skyhoundz series. In that way — assuming our business became successful — we would never have to worry from year-to-year about whether we could afford to continue a national series as originally envisioned by Lander. We believed that the Skyhoundz series could also serve as the tether that could tie the past and the future of our sport together…one that could preserve elements of the original contest series while moving in exciting new directions. We felt that, in order to move forward, we had to cut our ties to traditional sources of sponsorship and take a bold gamble. And so we did.

Alex Stein and "Ashley Whippet."

In 2001, we were set to stage the World Championship in Washington, DC, on the 15th of September. Competitors were winging their way to D.C. from places as far away as Japan when, without warning, the worst national tragedy in many of our lifetimes occurred. With air travel in the U.S. shut down, and the country in mourning, we quickly notified competitors that the World Championship would be rescheduled to a later date. One month later, on October 20 we held the first Hyperflite Skyhoundz World Championship in Atlanta. Twelve competitors competed in the Open Division and David Bootes & *Chico* won the World Championship.

Without sponsorship, finances were tight and we held our Awards Banquet in Hyperflite's small warehouse in midtown Atlanta. About 30 competitors, spouses and friends attended. Accommodations in the warehouse were spartan to say the least. During the banquet, thunderstorms hammered the Atlanta area and the power failed. The flicker of candlelight reflecting off the nearby boxes of Hyperflite discs was not exactly the ambiance that we wanted for our world finalists, but it was the best we could do under the circumstances.

It had been a trying year for us. Our inability to secure a major sponsor forced us to cut corners and make many sacrifices. We could not do all that we wanted to make the World Championship everything that it should have been. However, the competitors, with warmth and kindness, continued to support us. We resolved to work as hard as possible to reward their loyalty.

Today, the Hyperflite Skyhoundz World Canine Disc Championship Series is the largest and most well-attended canine disc competition series in the world. Competitors compete for World Championship titles in four distinct divisions — MicroDog, Open, Pairs Freestyle, and Sport. For those fortunate enough to qualify, the World Championship is truly a once-in-a-lifetime experience.

Jeff Perry

Hyperflite Skyhoundz World Canine Disc Championship trophies.

Getty

Budweiser

THIS BUD'S FOR YOU.

Jackie Nickerson

"Wizard" performed at Shea Stadium for the
New York Mets when he was less than one year old.

Dog grabs disc, human grabs dog!

Getting Started

Chapter 4

Getting started with canine disc play means finding the perfect dog. If you already have a dog, then congratulations are in order. Your family pet is a perfect companion for canine disc play. That may seem like a surprising statement. But, if you are like most dog owners, right at your feet sits a loving companion that wants to please you and likely prefers your company to just about anything with notable exceptions reserved for food, water, and an occasional romantic inkling toward the opposite sex.

If you don't have a dog already, then consider an animal shelter canine or a rescue dog. We have said for years that animal shelter mutts make great disc dogs. Most shelters offer beautiful dogs for little or no money. The all-American mutt can be a great selection as long as he has the mental and physical attributes necessary for participation in vigorous athletic activity. Saving a dog from the pound can be an especially rewarding experience.

If your heart is set on a purebred dog, check with local rescue organizations first. Many rescue organizations are breed specific and were created by enthusiasts of that specific breed. For example, there have been many purebred Border Collies purchased by people who fell in love with the breed, only to discover that such high-energy

The perfect dog for you is waiting patiently at a local animal shelter.

Jeff Perry

Sven Van Driessche

Mike and Kathy Miller performing in Pairs Freestyle (See "Gravy" story at right).

canines are not always compatible with small children. And, it's not just high-energy breeds like Border Collies that have breed-specific rescue organizations. Pretty much any breed has such groups. They may not be local, but if you check the internet, you will probably find most breeds represented.

If you have never owned or cared for a dog before, then you must understand that pet ownership, or stewardship, as some prefer to call it, is a responsibility that should not be taken lightly. With proper care, many canines can live to be 16 years old and they will require regular care and attention, especially as they age. You may not be a good candidate for a dog if you travel a lot, or if you will be relocating to a foreign country. Quarantines and cultural issues may make it difficult for you to take your pet with you when you move. The possibility of military service should also make one think twice before acquiring a pet.

If you are considering getting a dog for a child, then you should be prepared to be responsible for the dog, if, as frequently happens, the child is not mature enough to handle the full-time responsibility. Keep in mind that your dog will depend on you for shelter, health care, food, entertainment and love for its lifetime. And please don't suffer from the misconception that dogs are inexpensive to care for. Canine veterinary care can be nearly as costly as human care for many procedures. If you're not sure about where you are in life or whether you will have the time and money to take care of a pet for many years to come, then consider volunteering to foster a dog through your local animal shelter or humane society. Not only will these organizations be thankful for your efforts, you will also learn much from the experience.

Despite these cautions, you can be absolutely certain that your pet will give you, in love, ten times the investment of your time or energy in caring for it.

SELECTING A DOG

First and foremost, understand that there is no guarantee that the particular dog that you choose will have aptitude for, or interest in, canine disc play. We always say that you can teach almost any canine to catch a flying disc. And you can…almost. Once in a blue moon, a canine may have absolutely no interest in disc play and nothing you or anyone else can do seems to change that unfortunate reality. You must always be prepared for that possibility. Even if your canine does take to the disc, he may not be the star athlete that you hoped for. Just remember that a dog is for life and although you might not be blessed with a great disc dog, you will be blessed with a loving companion who idolizes you despite your faults.

In selecting a canine it is always best to choose one that is suited to your particular lifestyle. If you already have pets then you

GRAVY

About 10 years ago our club, the K9 Aircorps, was in San Bernardino, California doing a yearly disc dog show for an organization known as "Dream Street" that puts on summer camps for terminally ill children all over the country.

At events like this, one of the things I enjoy doing is teaching the youngsters simple trick sequences. So, with my dog "Pro" in front of me, I showed the kids how I make "Pro" run between my legs and circle back around to catch the disc. They watched as I tapped my right leg, to make "Pro" circle right, and then my left leg to make him circle left.

While teaching this move to a group of about a dozen kids, I noticed one little boy in the distance, with disc in hand, mimicking my moves. I had been told he was shy and would probably not want to throw to the dog. However, he did watch all the other children try the trick sequence.

We finished up our play session and, as I was chatting with the doctors and nurses that care for the children, I glanced toward my dog. The shy little boy had somehow made his way over to "Pro" without any of us noticing!

We all watched in horror as the young boy — whose legs were not quite as long as "Pro" was tall — set his feet and tapped his right leg. Bang! "Pro" was off like a gunshot, which surprised the boy. His eyes were as big as eggs as "Pro" raced between his little legs and made the turn. The little boy's feet came off the ground as "Pro" squeezed under him and you could see pure fear in the boy's eyes. When "Pro" looked up for the disc, it wasn't there. In a reflex action, the boy threw the disc in the air.

As I started for the boy, with doctors and nurses right behind me, the boy picked up a second disc, smiled broadly and did the trick a second time in the opposite direction. Again, "Pro" lifted the boy off the ground as he ran between the boy's legs, and the boy — better prepared this time — made a perfect throw to "Pro." The boy then picked up his disc and walked off the field wearing a proud smile. The doctors turned and said, "You're coming back next year aren't you?" Easy answer!

— Mike Miller (and Kathy Miller)
Skyhoundz Lifetime Achievement Award Recipient(s)

must consider the impact that a new addition to the family will have on those canine family members. Introduce any canine that you are considering to your existing menagerie in a neutral setting and observe how they behave. Even if everything goes smoothly, be sure that you have the ability to return the candidate canine if things don't work out once you get home.

Each purebred or mixed-breed canine has different physical and mental characteristics as well as certain inherited qualities and weaknesses including size, speed, stamina, leaping ability and intensity. The same qualities that make a great herding, sporting or retrieving canine, may make for a great disc dog, but not necessarily a wonderful family pet. For example, Australian Shepherds, with their inexhaustible supply of energy and intensity can make phenomenal disc dogs. Unfortunately, these dogs may not be a good fit in families with small children since their strong herding instincts might cause them to herd and nip the wee ones as they might sheep!

Don't forget to consider the characteristics generally associated with a particular breed. Canines with long snouts and long legs, have a better chance of catching a flying disc than snub-nosed dogs or toy breeds which are not well suited to disc play because of their physical limitations.

PRO TIP

Common Things We Do To De-Motivate Our Dogs — In disc dog training we often talk about how to motivate our dogs to do certain things. But very little attention is paid to the things that we do to de-motivate them. Far too many times we sabotage our motivation training without even realizing it. Sensitive dogs are especially easy to de-motivate as they are extremely aware of the moods and subtle behaviors of their human counterparts. So what are some of the things we humans do to de-motivate our dogs?

Sighing and/or Groaning — A well-timed wooohoo! can motivate our dogs, but an equally well-timed (and often involuntary) sigh or groan for a missed catch can have the opposite effect.

Body Tension — As we become uptight and tense up our bodies, our dogs sense this and begin to feel as if they have somehow done something to cause our stress which in turn de-motivates them. And don't think you can mask your tension by feigning enthusiasm. Your dog will know when you are faking it!

Tone of Voice — Carefully consider the impact that your tone of voice will have on your dog. Dogs often respond more to tone than to words. The right words spoken in the wrong tone can shut a dog down completely.

Confusion — It is important that we communicate our expectations clearly and consistently in order to avoid confusing our canines. Confusion leads to frustration which raises the stress level of our canines thereby de-motivating them.

Boredom — When training disc dogs, it is important that we don't obsessively train the same trick or move repeatedly. Many times we repeat tricks, not because our canines make mistakes, but because we aren't happy with our side of the equation. Maintaining variety as you train will help keep your canine eager and focused.

— Jackie Parkin, Hyperflite Skyhoundz World Finalist

Adult Border Collie attempting to train human child how to throw.

Once you make a selection, part of your responsibility as a dog owner and trainer is to learn to recognize and work with your dog's particular characteristics and special qualities. For example, a Hound will be a great tracker, a Working Dog will be tireless, a Pointer will be focused, etc. There are many excellent breed books available for investigating the characteristics of various breeds. The same characteristics applicable to purebred canines will be found in mixed-breed shelter mutts in varying degrees. The experienced shelter staff will often be able to hazard an educated guess as to the likely breeding of the dogs that are available for adoption. This information coupled with your own experience and observations will help you find a dog that will be a good disc dog and a great family pet.

THE M.U.T.T.S. TEST

A helpful tool that you can use in your search is the *MUTTS Test* for disc dog aptitude: MUTTS is an acronym that stands for Mouth-Up-Tracking-Training, and Socialization.

Mouth — Does the tested canine use its mouth to playfully grab you, your clothes, a tug toy, a ball, etc. An oral fixation is a sure sign of disc dog aptitude since a canine must be comfortable holding and grabbing a disc in its mouth. Examine the canine's teeth for any dental or gum problem and as a crude method of determining a canine's age.

Up — Everyone loves to watch a dog jump high and make a mid-air catch of a disc in flight. Consequently, "up" is where we want to see potential disc dogs go. At the animal shelter, pay attention as you approach kennels. The good jumpers quickly show themselves as they bounce with excitement at the arrival of a stranger in the kennel area. Thinner canines with longer limbs will frequently be the best jumpers but sometimes the chunky ones will surprise you.

Tracking — Does your disc dog candidate track or chase objects that roll along the ground and, perhaps even attempt to grab them? If so, then the battle is half won. Many canines will follow your hand or a ball, disc, or other toy if you move it rapidly within their field of vision. Good disc dogs are adept at focusing on moving objects and following them wherever they may go.

Training — Disc dogs need to be trainable not only when the leash is on, but also when they are off-leash at great distances from their owners. While it is difficult to determine the trainability of a particular canine in a brief visit, you can stack the odds in your favor by attempting to teach the candidate canine a basic obedience command such as *sit*. Perhaps your candidate will immediately sit when you give the *sit* command which will tell you that, not only is your dog trainable...he may already be trained to a degree. If the dog looks at you as if you are speaking a foreign language (which you are), then give the *sit* command and gently press the rear end of the canine toward the ground while simultaneously lifting gently on its collar. Reward the dog with praise when it finally sits. Then try it again. After a few attempts, the canine should begin to sit on its own when your hand touches its hind quarters. Some dogs learn faster than others but you want to see some tangible indication that the canine is trying to figure out what it is that you want it to do. A vacant stare or a stubborn refusal to do as you wish may mean either that the animal is not the best candidate for Disc Dog 101 or that you have inadvertently wandered into the feline section of the shelter!

Socialization — Disc dogs, even more than the typical family pet, must demonstrate a favorable disposition toward humans and other animals. Disc dogs are frequently in close proximity to people and dogs when they are off-leash and it simply won't do to have a canine that expresses aggression toward

others. Overly-aggressive canines can be handled by expert trainers but are a headache that mere mortals should seek to avoid. Watch how your candidate relates to the dogs in the nearby kennels. If possible, ask the shelter to arrange a play session while other male and female canines of comparable size are in the vicinity. Carefully observe the manner in which the candidate canine interacts with other canines and people. Finally, if you have small children, you will want to find a canine with a high level of tolerance toward youngsters.

The *MUTTS test* can be given to any dog or puppy and, when coupled with common sense and intuition, the *MUTTS test* can be a useful tool to help you find a fun companion. Finally, although many people assume that only mixed-breeds can be found at animal shelters, a substantial number of purebred dogs can be found there as well.

GENERAL CHARACTERISTICS OF POPULAR DISC DOG BREEDS

The canine of today originated from the ancient wolf of the past. For more

Future Canadian disc dogger.

Jeff Perry

Peter Bloeme

I don't know whether to drink it, or take a bath in it.

than 1,000 years, canines with specific traits have been bred for protection, hunting, herding, and other tasks. The following compilation of characteristics associated with different breed groups may aid you in selecting the canine best suited to your personality and lifestyle. Additionally, many mixed-breed canines may possess the characteristics of their parents — which may actually increase their aptitude for disc dog play. Imagine the speed of a Whippet paired with the intensity of a Border Collie, or the retrieving capability of a Labrador combined with the intelligence of a Poodle. Of course, these combinations may not produce the ideal disc dog — whatever that is — but the possibilities do make shelter canines worth a serious look.

While on the subject of mixed-breed dogs we want to strongly discourage anyone from trying to breed canines — especially mixed-breed canines — in the hope of creating the ultimate disc dog. There are already enough accidents at your local shelter and you certainly don't want to contribute to the pet overpopulation problem

with an experiment gone awry.

There now exist more than 400 recognized dog breeds. Breeds sharing certain characteristics are placed in groups including Herding, Hound, Terrier, Toy, Sporting, and Working, with each group containing a minimum of 18 different breeds. The characteristics of some of these breed groups are as follows:

Herding — Herding breeds share the unique trait of being able to direct and control the movement of other animals. This can be accomplished through staring (The Eye), sudden or rapid movement, and even by nipping or physically grabbing the animal being herded. Herding canines range in size from the relatively small Welsh Corgi up to the comparatively large Belgian Malinois. Other well-known breeds in this group include Australian Cattle Dogs, Australian Shepherds, Belgian Tervurens, German Shepherds, and Border Collies.

Hound — Hounds are known for their hunting skills. Some hounds have incredible scenting powers, tracking skills, or the tremendous stamina necessary to run down prey. Other hounds are known for the baying sound that they make as they hunt or track their prey. That sound, most familiar to the occasional escaped convict, means that the con's brief vacation from the Big House is almost over. Are there small hounds you might ask? Just think Beagle…and hold your hands over your ears! Some other well-known breeds in this group include the Bloodhound, Dachshund, Greyhound, and Whippet.

Terrier — Many terrier owners think canines in this group should be known as *terrors* instead of Terriers due to their intensity and energy. In addition to their energy, Terriers have quite distinctive personalities. Terriers — originally bred to hunt and kill rats, rabbits, and other small mammals — are small, feisty, highly determined, and typically possessed of short-hair. Some well known Terrier breeds include the Airedale Terrier, Cairn Terrier, Miniature Schnauzer, Smooth Fox Terrier, and Staffordshire Bull Terrier.

Toy — Much to the chagrin of larger-sized canines, toy breeds are not merely their personal play things but are instead…actual canines capable of vigorous participation in disc dog sports. Toys are typically bred as companions for those residing in small apartments and often are seen being carried around by celebrities. These smaller canines generally weigh less than 10 pounds and are relatively inexpensive to care for. Historically, Toy breeds haven't performed as well as their larger brethren in canine disc competitions. However, all that changed when Hyperflite added a MicroDog Division to the Skyhoundz World Championship Series thereby giving smaller canines the opportunity to win their own championship title. Some-well known breeds in the Toy group include the Chihuahua, Italian Greyhound, Maltese, Papillion, Pomeranian, Pug, and Yorkshire Terrier.

Sporting — Sporting dogs are known for hunting, tracking, and retrieving. Canines in the Sporting Group are friendly, good-natured, high-energy dogs. Some well-known breeds in this group include the Brittany Spaniel, Golden Retriever, Irish Setter, Labrador Retriever, and Pointer.

Working — Working dogs perform jobs like guarding property, protecting their owners, pulling sleds, and water rescue. The dogs in this group are typically large and imposing dogs. Some well-known Working dog breeds include the Akita, Boxer, Great Dane, Rottweiler, Saint Bernard, and Siberian Husky.

It bears repeating that the dog you select, whether from an animal shelter or a top breeder, may not turn out to be a champion disc dog despite your best efforts. If that happens, then you still

We humans aren't the only ones fighting the battle of the bulge. Canine obesity is a serious problem. Overweight canines, in addition to being more prone to injury, face a higher risk of developing ailments like heart and respiratory disease. Excess weight can also worsen arthritis and lead to diabetes mellitus. It's never too late to make lifestyle changes for your canine that include proper nutrition, appropriate caloric intake, and regular exercise. An active and properly fed canine, in addition to being happier, will also live longer.

It's important to let puppies be puppies and not overdo your disc training. Of course, teething on a buddy, can be painful. Ouch!

Peter Bloeme

SAFETY AND HEALTH CONSIDERATIONS

Immediately after acquiring a new dog, get him a collar with the proper identification imprinted including his name, your name, your address and your cell phone number (In case you become separated from your canine while traveling). Have him wear the collar at all times, even in the house. If, by accident, you become separated from your dog, an identification tag could be a lifesaver. Also consider an implantable microchip identifier. Microchips have reunited many grateful dogs with their humans.

Since it is imperative that your dog be healthy before attempting any strenuous disc activity, check with your veterinarian before starting out. Have your pet examined regularly. Keep your dog's immunizations (such as Rabies, Parvo, Kennel Cough) current. Have your dog tested for Heartworm regularly and keep him on a monthly preventative. Remember, your dog can't tell you if he have a great family pet that will love you and try its hardest to please you. What could be better than that?

isn't feeling well, so you must develop the ability to assess his physical and mental condition. Learn to be observant. Notice whether or not your dog is eating properly and check his stools for any unusual discharges or worms.

While petting your dog, you may feel bumps, growths, or lacerations. Have anything unusual checked by your veterinarian.

Fleas are a problem, especially in warmer climates, but with flea shampoos and monthly topical treatments, the life cycle of fleas can be broken thereby aiding in their control. We do not recommend the use of flea collars, though. Many veterinarians believe that flea collars may do more harm than good. If you do decide to use one, at least remove the collar when giving your dog a bath or letting him swim. The flea-killing chemicals used are intensified by water and are concentrated around your dog's head. Your money will be better spent on monthly topical treatments for your canine and room foggers and sprays to control fleas in, and around, your house.

TEETHING AND CANINE ORAL HYGIENE

If your disc dog in training happens to be a puppy, then prepare yourself for the nightmare of teething. Take this as a warning — a pup is like an infant and will put everything and anything into its mouth. The key difference is that infants don't have shark-like teeth that can tear through virtually anything including exactly one shoe out of every pair in your house!

What you can do to minimize the fallout during this difficult period is to buy chew-toys (by the gross if necessary), including rubber bones, balls, etc. Hyperflite *Jawz Pup discs*, while not designed for such use, will also serve well as nearly indestructible chew toys and they also double nicely as food and water dishes for your toothy monster. If you think your dog will like it — get it. However, do not give your dog an old pair of shoes or socks. Think of it this way: How is your dog going to know an old pair of shoes from a favorite new pair? Avoid giving your dog real bones as these can cause severe intestinal block-

Hey guys, a little more chewing and I'll have the combination to this leash figured out!

age or damage due to splintering. Also, never let your puppy chew anything that it can damage because small rubber, plastic or leather pieces can lodge in your pup's intestines and cause serious injury or worse.

Always, keep an eye on your dog when he is chewing. It is easy to assume that your dog is happily chewing on something you approve of, until you look down and find out it simply isn't so. The genetic makeup of puppies suggests anything within mouth range is fair game. Can you help it if that item happens to be a 220-volt air conditioner cord? The answer is yes, we hope.

It is important for puppy teeth to come in and drop out naturally so that adult teeth can fill the gaps normally. Make sure that your puppy toys are not so hard that they can damage your pup's teeth. Incidentally, your dog's teeth will need to be cleaned by a veterinarian periodically, as dogs can develop gum disease similar to humans. Regular cleanings will prevent early tooth decay and subsequent tooth loss. Some people actually brush their dog's teeth. And, we've been told that many dogs don't have to be held down in headlocks and

You never know what you can find inside a bag...

Boy, that's a tight fit.

Jeff Hoot

This type of liquid nutrition for adults, while making a poor score in competition more palatable, is not recommended for your canine friend.

healthy teeth. Although the use of dry food, dog biscuits and chews can reduce the speed and amount of tartar build-up, regular cleanings, performed under anesthesia by your veterinarian, will keep your pet's teeth and gums healthy.

NUTRITION

Experts in the field of nutrition assert that a healthy and balanced diet can prevent many health problems for people. Dog's are no different. Since you are responsible for your dog's health, you must select a nutritious and healthy canine diet that will complement your dog's athletic lifestyle. As news reports have shown, the premium brands are not necessarily immune from contamination by toxins and chemicals.

Here are some things to keep in mind as you seek sustenance for your pet. First, a poor diet can seriously harm your dog's health and shorten its life span. The best food for your dog is not necessarily the most expensive, as nutritional quality does not always go hand-in-hand with price. Carefully research the brand of food that you are considering. Avoid foods that contain animal by-products (read — slaughterhouse waste), preservatives (read — potentially cancer-causing chemicals), or fillers (read — your guess is as good as ours).

There is a nascent movement underway that suggests that perhaps the healthiest diet is one not entirely unlike a human diet. A diet composed of meat, fruit, grains and vegetables, some would assert, may be the best canine diet of all. Of course, those who advocate a human-like diet for canines are careful to point out that we should avoid the salt and condiments and fattening things that make food palatable for us humans. Also, if you do choose to feed

that they actually enjoy the tooth attention. We'll let you be the judge.

When your dog is an adult, his teeth can wear down with play. Dirty tennis balls, fabric discs and older-style plastic discs with deep grooves can trap grit that can act like revolving sandpaper on canine teeth. Avoid playing with any toy that you can't keep largely free of dirt and grit. Some tooth wear is normal and not something to be overly concerned about, but have your veterinarian monitor the condition of your dog's teeth and watch for excessive wear. Your vet can also check your canine for tartar build-up. Tartar can be seen as a hard, yellow coating on a dog's normally white teeth. It causes canine gums to become red and inflamed and leads to gum disease that can in turn lead to the loss of

Does this mean I have to brush my teeth again?

your pet human food, make sure to only give it de-boned meats. Meat bones can be particularly deadly to canines. Never feed them to your pet or allow your pet to chew on them. The internet is a great way to find do-it-yourself recipes for canine diets as well as to learn about companies that prepare custom diets, using human ingredients, for pets with food allergies or special needs. Do your own research and draw your own conclusions. Your pet will be healthier for your efforts.

Whatever you choose to feed your canine, above all, do not overfeed your dog. A trim animal will be able to participate in vigorous athletic activity with less strain on joints, muscles, tendons and ligaments. Endurance will be enhanced as will your dog's quickness and leaping agility.

More pet owners doom their animals to disease and early deaths by overfeeding than from any other cause. Never free-feed your dog! In other words, don't make an abundant supply of food available to your dog for snack-

You don't need to be a genius to spot an overweight dog.

Launching for the catch!

Jay Moldow

Christopher Vitale showcasing "Bear's" new trim figure...see the "Pro Tip" below.

ing at your pet's whim. There are no excuses for a fat dog! While we may have a hard time controlling what goes into our mouths, we certainly can regulate what goes into the mouths of our canines. Dogs still have some of their old instincts such as thinking they need to eat all they can whenever they can. They beg and look forlorn. Don't give in!

You should be able to run your hands over your dog's rib cage and feel ribs. There should also be some definition between your dog's rib cage and his abdomen. Check with your veterinarian for more guidance on the proper weight for your athletic canine. Your dog should not bear even a passing resemblance to a 50-gallon drum with legs!

At Hyperflite disc dog training clinics, we frequently encounter overweight canines. Owners often comment that they are feeding their canines exactly what the dog food company recommends. And, naturally, we hear *my dog's veterinarian says my dog's weight is fine.* These statements don't really surprise us because dog food companies are in the business of selling dog food and veterinarians don't want to offend some of their best customers by telling them that their children are fat! Without exception, when people take our advice to heart and make an effort to slim down their overweight canines, both dog and owner are happier for the effort.

Whether your dog competes or just plays hard, it is better for him to be on a consistent feeding schedule. Regulated feedings allow you to monitor how much your dog eats and also help with

PRO TIP

Several years ago, my dog "Bear" wasn't performing well and getting injured often. After a Regional competition, an experienced disc dogger approached me and told me how much he liked my dog, but that "Bear" could use to lose a few pounds. When I asked how many, he said, "perhaps 10 lbs!" After I put "Bear" on a diet he seemed healthier and happier and he performed much better on the playing field. And, he even looked better.

— Christopher Vitale, Hyperflite Skyhoundz World Finalist

Peter Bloeme

Believe it or not, this is not a "vaulting" catch.

housebreaking. In order to keep blood sugar and energy levels consistent, some choose to feed their canines one small meal, twice daily. Feed your canine at least one-hour before or one-hour after exercise to minimize the chance of a condition sometimes referred to as *twisted gut*, a blockage of the stomach which can be fatal to canines.

When feeding your pet, and at all other times, make sure water is available to your pet. In the summer, place your dog's water bowl in a cool or shady area because water left in the hot sun can easily become too hot to drink.

Finally, on the subject of treats, many ordinary humans falsely assume that disc doggers use treats to teach their canines tricks. To the contrary, disc doggers know that the best reward for a disc dog is another throw! Your dog will perform because he loves you, loves what he does and appreciates your praise.

NAMING YOUR DOG

When you are ready to choose a name for your pet, give it some thought. Remember, your dog will have that name for the rest of his life. Many new dog owners labor for days before settling on the perfect name. Choose an easy-to-pronounce name of no more than three syllables if possible. Avoid names that sound like obedience commands for obvious reasons. Over the years, we have seen some doozies including: *Bigger than a Chigger* (*Chigger* for short) and *The Mighty Carolina Hurricane* (*Hurricane* if anyone asks). Disc doggers are quite clever. A cursory survey of canine names from recent Hyperflite Skyhoundz Regional Qualifiers reads like a Kentucky Derby race card: There's *Karma, Cheeky, Nacho, Ruckus, Sprite, Buzzard, Zulu, Spinner, Freckles, Speckles, Nova, Happy Girl, Captain Jack, Jumpin' Jack, One-Eyed Jack, Harley Davidson, White Lightnin', Cookie, Wookie, Jedi, Obi, Whoopin' Roo, Party Boy Ace, Glory, Rory,*

A jumping grab of a "Jawz disc."

Bayer (a headache for its owner perhaps!), Big Air Buster, Bullet, Arrow, Nitro, Rocket, Guinness, Foster, Killian, Bud, Maverick, Spur, Dasher, Comet, Allie Oop, Pixie Chick, Scooby Snack, Murphy Brown, Beamer, Mercedes, Red Bone, Iggy Pop, Five, Six, Seven and Wigglebutt 7 of 9. The only limit — your imagination and, hopefully, good taste. Remember, it won't do to name your pet something that would make a competition announcer blush!

GROOMING

Grooming is very important for your dog's health and appearance. The effort needed to groom your dog depends entirely on the breed you have. Therefore, we suggest that you ask your veterinarian or a groomer for specifics. Certain thick coated breeds will benefit from a summer cut. This type of cut keeps long-haired breeds cooler during the warm months and keeps doggie-hair tumbleweeds from blowing through your house or apartment. Please note that a summer cut is not the same as a crew cut which can expose a canine's skin to the sun, biting flies, and mosquitoes. An experienced groomer will help you choose a cut that's right for your dog.

Brush dogs several times a week and, while so doing, take a moment to simultaneously examine their coats for ticks and fleas, their ears for dirt and mite infestations and, finally, check their nails and trim as necessary. Although super-active dogs will self-trim their nails through friction with rough surfaces like the ground, many dogs will need regular trimming of their dew claws (thumbs) and nails. Claws that are too long can be torn or injured. Long claws can also injure you if you do tricks that put you in close contact with your dog. To trim your dog's nails you will need canine nail clippers which are available at any pet store. If your dog has translucent nails, you can see the quick...the darker or pinkish area inside the nail. Your dog's nails need clipping when they extend much beyond the quick. Do not cut your dog's nails to the quick, which is painful to your canine and may cause bleeding or infection. If you aren't sure how to trim your dog's nails, ask your veterinarian

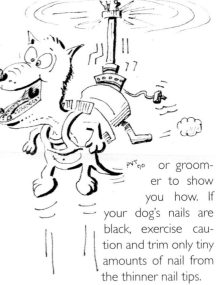

or groomer to show you how. If your dog's nails are black, exercise caution and trim only tiny amounts of nail from the thinner nail tips.

Bathe your dog when it looks (or smells!) like he needs it, though normally not more than twice a month, or so. Bathing too frequently can lead to dry skin. If you decide to jump in the tub or shower as you bathe your pet, you might want to wear a swimsuit. You'll just have to trust us on this one.

With "vaults" timing is everything.

It's not often you see a trainer jumping higher than a disc dog.

Obedience Training
Chapter 5

A FOUNDATION OF OBEDIENCE

Basic obedience training is crucial to the development and happiness of any family pet. Just as every building needs a strong foundation, your canine needs a foundation of obedience training upon which to build a relationship with you and your family. You can't expect to control your dog on the playing field, or at a public park, without a practical grasp of basic commands.

Additionally, even if your canine already knows basic verbal commands, to really control your canine like a pro, you must also teach your dog hand signals that it can respond to when it is too far away to hear your verbal commands. As you begin to train your canine, be sure to give consistent hand gestures in combination with verbal commands so that you don't have to teach these later on when your canine may be more set in its ways.

Always keep obedience and disc play fun and safe for your dog.

If you've never trained a dog before then you and your canine should take an obedience class together. Obedience classes are not just for dogs and you can expect to learn as much as, if not more than, your dog. An additional benefit of obedience classes is the structure they provide; namely, regularly scheduled opportunities to train together without the usual distractions found at home. An important side benefit of obedience classes will be that your canine will have regular opportunities to socialize with the other dogs in your class in a carefully-controlled environment. Visit your local pet retailer to find an obedience class near you. Try and meet or talk to your instructor before your class and make sure that the instructor has a philosophy of training that meets with your expectations. If you don't like what you hear, then find a new instructor. You can also fly solo,

Peter Bloeme

Lightning rod for disc dog fun...

Thom Gillott

Faster than a speeding bullet.

if you wish, and there are a number of excellent training books and guides that will help you make the most of your relationship with your canine. If you do train your dog on your own, then set aside regular blocks of time to work with your canine. Don't let cell phones or other distractions cut into the quality training time that you and your pet need. Progress will come slowly unless you regularly devote time to a training regimen.

Although an obedience training treatise is beyond the scope of *Disc Dogs!*, some general tips and suggestions will prove useful.

As you begin training your puppy or older canine be mindful of certain guiding principles that we call the *Four P's* — Praise, Patience, Persistence and Phun!

Praise — As you begin your obedience training, whether or not you use treats to reinforce behavior, remember to lavish praise on your canine when the desired result is achieved. At the beginning, even a small step in the right direction is deserving of praise. Our pets really do want to please us and it is amazing

> **PRO TIP**
> *Although food treats are often used in training they are not essential. A moment of playtime, or a quick toss of a favorite toy, coupled with enthusiastic and animated praise, are far more effective than treats in reinforcing a desired behavior.*
>
> *— Jeff Stanaway, 2003 Hyperflite Skyhoundz World Champion*

how excited they get when they do something that makes us happy.

Patience — Only a rare canine will race through obedience training and graduate with high honors. Most of the others move along at varying speeds. In fact, dogs are *like a box of chocolates* as Forrest Gump might say, *you really never know what you're going to get.* However, even though dogs learn at different speeds, they all eventually *get it* as long as we are patient with them as they try to understand our desires while they simultaneously learn our language.

Persistence — Obedience training is not an occasional thing. It requires a commitment on your part to attend all of your obedience classes and practice between classes so you don't fall behind. You will be rewarded handsomely, throughout the life of your canine for the extra effort that you put in during the formative early stages of your relationship with your best friend.

Phun! — Expect that your canine will not be thrilled at the prospect of doing unusual things like walking by

Praise is very important in training your dog.

your side as you rapidly turn, stop and change directions (heeling) or staying in one place while you walk away from him (sit-stay). This doggie drudgery is made so much better if you make the experience fun for your canine. Bring a favorite tug toy, disc or ball and take a break every now and again and reward your dog for a job well done. If your canine associates training sessions with fun, then you are more likely to keep his attention as you practice boring and repetitive tasks.

"Gilbert" patiently waiting in a down position.

Catching isn't just for the dogs...

Sven Van Duessche

BASIC OBEDIENCE COMMANDS

In almost any basic obedience class you will learn at least five or six key obedience commands.

Come — A canine immediately comes to the trainer when recalled with the *come* command. Normal application — a recall command that is given to compel a return of the canine to the trainer. Canine Disc Application — a recall command given to expedite a return to the trainer, often with urgency, *come, come, come,* often accompanied by a *hurry* command.

Down — Normally from a sitting position, but also from a standing position, the canine lays down with all four paws in contact with the ground. Normal Application — This is a resting position for a canine. Canine Disc Application — This is the typical start position for long distance throws. The *down* command also precedes the *roll* command which is used in many disc dog trick sequences.

Heel — A canine's shoulders are parallel to the legs of the trainer, normally, on a chosen side of the trainer's body. The chosen side, once selected, is not varied. Normal Application — An aid to leash-walking a canine. Canine Disc Application — Heeling is always performed off leash and is used in a variety of Freestyle trick sequences especially when a canine is moving around and between the legs of a thrower.

No — Although not normally part of a basic obedience curriculum, the command *no* which most dogs learn if they learn nothing else, is typically taught in basic obedience

classes, either by design, or by necessity. The *no* command should cause your dog to immediately cease whatever it is doing and wait for further instruction. This command could save your dog's life! A firm *no* can stop a well-trained canine from walking out into a busy road, eating something harmful, or playing with a dangerous wild animal.

Sit — On command, the canine lowers its haunches to the ground in a sitting position. Normal application — This is a canine semi-resting position that is used when leash walking a dog. Canine Disc Application — The sit position is an essential ready position that a canine assumes before various trick sequences are initiated including *backflips, vaults, juggling,* butterfly tosses, etc.

Stay — The canine remains in place in a sitting, standing or down position until recalled by the *come* command. Normal Application: The *stay* command keeps a canine in a particular location for extended periods of time. Canine Disc Application — The *stay* command is a positioning command that is used to allow a trainer to prepare for a trick sequence that requires proper spacing between the canine and thrower.

Lawrence Frederick and "Aero Dynamic."

Stays are always brief during competition where time is of the essence.

ADVANCED
OBEDIENCE COMMANDS

As you progress with obedience training, additional more advanced commands may be added to your canine's vocabulary and all of them have potential application to disc dog play or competition.

Drop —This useful command can be used whenever *Scruffey* grabs a prohibited item or tries to eat something unpleasant. In canine disc sports it is an essential command because it is a rare canine that can catch a disc in its mouth when another disc already occupies the same real estate.

Go — This command, though not a standard in obedience training, is exceedingly useful for disc dogs. It is the typical start command for a variety of tricks and, especially, long-distance throws. Position your dog a few paces behind the start line, give the *go* command, and you're off to the races!

Kennel — Dogs that are kennel trained at an early age often willingly enter their kennels upon hearing the *kennel* command. Indeed, kennel-trained canines grow to think of their kennels as a safe place and often nap in them of their own volition. Canines introduced to the kennel for the first time at an airport just before a terrifying first flight on an airliner develop quite an aversion to these plastic torture chambers. Start early with kennel training and your life will be considerably easier.

Leave it — This command is the thinking dog's version of *no*. It is a more specific command than *no* and means, depending upon the circumstances — *Don't chase the kids! Don't eat the kids! Don't eat another dog's food! Don't eat my food, etc.!*

Roll — This command is not a particularly practical command — unless your canine catches on fire! However, disc doggers use the *roll* command in trick sequences just to jazz things up a bit.

Speak — Teaching the *speak* command is as easy as saying the word repeatedly when your canine barks and rewarding a bark with praise and a moment of play time. Eventually your dog will figure it out. But, make sure your dog has a firm grasp of the *no* command before it learns to **speak!** Although there is debate about whether you should encourage barking, it can offer a cute moment during a disc dog routine and it might save your life if your *crib* ever catches fire.

Spin — This maneuver is the classic dog chasing its tail trick and like the *roll* command it is frequently used to add some visual interest to disc dog routines. Border Collies, for some unknown reason, spin almost instinctively while other canines actually have to be taught to spin.

Take — This command is a fun one for canines. They get told to grab stuff with their mouths! Its use in canine disc play is widespread. Any time you want to initiate a trick whereby the canine takes the disc out of your hand, off of your body, or out of your mouth, you give the *take* command to initiate the desired action.

Wait—The *wait* command tells a dog that action is still imminent, but that patience is required. The dog should remain on alert until it receives another command.

With a proper foundation of obedience training, you can begin disc dog training with confidence and a high probability of success. It's only human to want your dog to be obedience trained and a disc star overnight, but patience is the key to success.

If you have a puppy, you will want to begin your puppy's education as early as possible, starting when your pup is as young as 3 months old. Remember to always train in a fun, friendly and relaxed manner. Your puppy will have a very short attention span, so plan accordingly. Training should seem like a big game. If your dog is younger than three months of age, then spend time bonding with your pup and avoid anything more serious than gentle play.

Kennels are a great place to relax and get away from life's pressures.

"Go" is good for sending your dog in distance events.

"Come" is especially necessary in off-leash work.

Even a "bow" command can be useful in Freestyle competitions.

As you begin training, bear in mind that consistency is of the utmost importance. Always use the same word to command a particular behavior. It's important not to confuse your dog with long, multi-syllable or multi-word commands. It's much easier for your dog to hear, differentiate and follow single-word commands. For example, say, *down*, not *Buster, please go lie down.*

Dog's can't easily interpret complete sentences so keep it simple for them.

BASIC TRAINING PHILOSOPHIES

Teaching a dog to catch a flying disc, or any complicated behavior for that matter, is an incremental process. To increase your chance of success, you must break the task into its smallest components. Liberally reward incremental progress toward the goal. Since canine disc tricks are typically more complicated to teach than the average obedience command many top trainers use a combination of methods to teach a particular move. Regardless of the method you use, remember to keep the experience fun for your canine. Any time you give your canine love, attention and praise he will continue to try and please you. He will work at figuring out exactly what it is that you want and will really try to understand what it is you are trying to teach him.

Again, it is important that you remember, as you begin obedience training, to reward your dog both verbally (by praising him) and physically (by petting him) and keep your training ses-

Bill Watters and "Air Major."

sions fun. Be animated in your interactions with your canine and keep your training sessions brief at first. Use treats if you must, but remember that you don't want your canine to expect treats as payment for services rendered. Even after your dog has perfected a command or trick, continue praising him to reinforce the behavior as well as reward him for his efforts.

A Word on Discipline

Never hit your dog! If your dog does not obey you, it is most likely your fault for not using the proper approach to teaching a particular behavior. Avoid expressing anger to your dog when it fails to grasp a command or trick that you are teaching. If you must, leave the room and pitch a quiet temper tantrum, yank out a gob of your own hair, or stomp up and down like a petulant child. But when you walk back into the room where your dog awaits you — with wagging tail — you better have a smile on your face! Anger is every bit as poisonous to a dog's soul as physi-

The "stay" command is a very useful command.

Len Silvester

cal violence. Save your anger for those occasions when it is justified. It is never justified when you are having fun with, or teaching, your pet.

We have become aware in recent years that there are trainers who advocate the use of shock collars and other pain or discomfort inflicting devices to discourage unwanted behavior. In our view, these devices are demonstrative of a lack of patience or poor training skills. If your obedience instructor recommends the use of these pain or discomfort inflicting devices, then our advice would be to find a new instructor. We realize that training can be occasionally frustrating, and sometimes it may seem as if your canine will never learn what you are trying to teach him, but it is both dangerous to your dog's

health and unlikely to encourage cooperation and understanding if you use pain as a teaching method.

You want a dog to respect you, not fear you. If you must punish your dog, there are various, safe methods such as using a stern vocal tone and level when appropriate. This form of correction usually works well. At the extreme, if your dog commits a serious offense, such as something that may endanger his life, you may have to resort to grabbing the fur on your dog's neck while gently shaking and scolding him. This is sometimes known as a scruff shake. This is apparently very similar to what a mother dog would do to scold a pup. It sounds a lot worse than it is, but it gets a dog's attention without actually harming him.

Jackie Bernard

Peter Bloeme teaching "Wizard" the "sit" command.

Jay Moldaw

Smile, then bite!

GRAVY

I had been thinking about finding a second dog for some time when, in the fall of 2005, I noticed a post on a disc dog bulletin board about a small Border Collie mix that was up for adoption. With a flip of a coin my decision was made — she would be my second disc dog. As I drove the nine hours from Kansas City to Indianapolis to meet her, I tried to come up with a name for number two. My other dog "KaCee," also a rescue dog, was named after Kansas City where I was originally from. As I was dreaming up names, I suddenly realized that I had somehow managed to wind up on a highway heading toward Chicago instead of Indianapolis. I took the next exit, and stopped at a rest stop to pick up a map.

At the exit I met a little old man who was having a hard time reading his own map. I chatted with him a bit and learned that he too was lost. He was trying to get to New Orleans to evacuate the rest of his family out of the city. Hurricane Katrina had just destroyed much of New Orleans and some of his family members were still there. After deciding that we both needed to head south, not north, we made our way back to our vehicles. When I saw his truck, I realized that it was marginally road safe and looked as if it were held together with bailing wire and rope. He had a truckload of supplies that he intended to drop off, and then he was packing up his family and getting them out of the city. After helping him re-wire one of his headlights, I filled up his tank with gas. I explained to him that this was my way of donating to the Hurricane Katrina relief effort. He was extremely grateful and he shook my hand and hugged me in thanks. When people hug you, you should at least know their names, so I asked him what his name was.

"Royal, my name is Royal Williams and it's a pleasure to meet you!" It was my pleasure to meet him as well. Now, some might call it coincidence…but being from Kansas City and meeting a man named "Royal" while I was on my way to pick up a dog that needed a name, struck me as being more like providence. And so "Royal," my new best buddy, was named after a really nice man who was doing a really nice thing."

— *Shaun Johnson, "KaCee" and "Royal"*

Some dogs just exude style when they play!

Flying Disc Basics

Chapter 6

Canine disc sports are a team effort. Although the focus is frequently on the canine, in order for your canine to shine on the playing field or at your local park, you must throw smoothly and accurately in a variety of weather conditions. Good throwers are not born though good throwing skills are most definitely born of hard work. Developing your throwing skills will enhance your dog's catching potential. We have often seen dogs with great natural abilities score poorly in competition solely because of the poor throwing skills of the human side of the equation.

It is amazing to watch a good dog suddenly blossom into a great dog when its human teammate works hard at becoming a good thrower. If you are new to canine disc sports, we recommend that you learn to throw, at least passably, before working with your dog. Good throwing skills will lessen the possibility of injury as well as keep your dog from becoming discouraged at the crucial early stage of your training.

Disc Selection

There are many flying discs on the market today. However, only certain discs are suitable for canine play.

For many years, the Fastback disc by the Wham-O Manufacturing Company was the required disc in competition. This was partly because of a sponsorship arrangement with the disc maker, but also because there were very few

At Hyperflite, we take our work seriously. Here, Jeff Perry learns how to use the hotstamp machine.

Peter Bloeme

Hyperflite's founders: Greg Perry, Peter Bloeme, and Jeff Perry

canine-sized discs suitable for canine competition. All that changed in 2000, when Hyperflite was founded.

For almost as long as we have been involved in canine disc sports, we have been keenly aware that a substantial number of canine disc competitors longed for a disc that was not easily damaged by canine teeth. Other competitors, hailing from northern states in the U.S., complained that their *Fastback discs* would crack or shatter in temperatures approaching 32 °F (freezing). These competitors would have to go to extreme measures to enjoy their favorite pastime when temperatures approached freezing.

We also observed that the throwing rings — the grip surface on the top of all Fastback discs, and the discs of most other manufacturers — tended to cap-

ture and hold dirt and grit which could then act like revolving sandpaper on the teeth of disc-catching canines.

When we (Peter Bloeme, Greg Perry, and Jeff Perry) formed Hyperflite, we resolved to address those issues and many others in any canine discs that we developed.

After months of design work, prototyping and rigorous testing, our fledgling company settled upon a disc design that we believed had the greatest potential to meet the needs of the modern canine athlete. The new disc design featured ultra low-profile grip surfaces on the top and bottom surfaces of the disc. These opposed grip surfaces allow the disc to be gripped easily, even when wet. Better still, the grip surfaces were shallow enough (less than 5/1000s of an inch) to help prevent the retention of

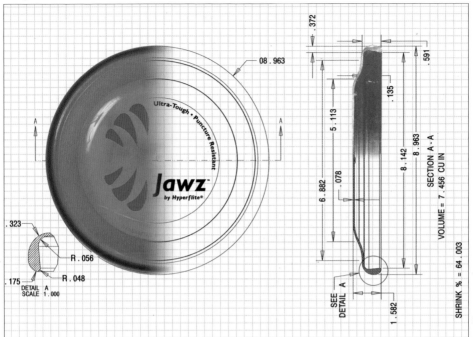

Engineering drawing of Hyperflite's "Jawz disc."

Peter Bloeme

dirt and grit. Grip surfaces on the prototype Hyperflite disc design were also considerably easier to clean than the v-grooved throwing rings on a Fastback disc which tend to grab and hold particulate matter. We named our new disc design the K-10 because it was more than any K-9 could ever hope for.

In addition to the tactile and dental issues discussed above, the Hyperflite K-10 was designed to be more stable and, consequently, easier to throw than any other disc used for canine play. And boy could the K-10 fly! Our tests with top throwers showed consistent 10 to 20% longer throws in all wind and weather conditions. Beginners commented that they could finally throw into the wind with the K-10 and experts loved that the inherent stability of the disc meant longer throws for their canines.

No detail was ignored with the K-10. In addition to the aerodynamic improvements, strength and durability were designed into the K-10 from the start. By reinforcing certain high-stress areas, we were able to lessen the possibility of rim cracks that can occur with tough biters.

Once the testing and refinement of the K-10 was completed, we applied for a U.S. Patent on the K-10 design. The patent application process was an expensive and time-consuming undertaking that drained our resources, both human and financial. Nevertheless, we felt that it was an important step that would allow us to continue to innovate without fear of infringement. With the patent applied for, we wasted no time in getting down to business.

First, we tackled a problem that has plagued canine owners for more than 30

Peter Bloeme

Just in time for the holidays!

years — disc longevity. Owners of Bulldog breeds and other tough biting canines could easily go through hundreds of discs each year just to participate in canine disc sports. Many competitors simply could not afford to participate in canine disc play because the cost of replacing discs was simply too great for them to bear. This was a wrong that we intended to rectify even if it meant that we wouldn't sell as many discs or make as much money in so doing. We believed then, as we believe now, that everyone, regardless of means, should be able to participate in canine disc play affordably.

Based on our research, we were certain that a polymer formulation could be developed that would be resistant to

Long Photography, Inc.

One of many reasons the "Jawz disc" was created.

Hyperflite Jawz Disc

formulation that appeared promising. The material held up well to testing on a mechanical testing device developed by Hyperflite and affectionately nicknamed *Hal K-9000* (think *2001 A Space Odyssey*) for its propensity to kill discs without remorse.

With the preliminary tests accomplished satisfactorily, the prototypes were subjected to real-world testing in the mouths of some of the most destructive canines on planet earth. The canine tests confirmed that this new material was, in fact, unbelievably resistant to damage from toothy canines. Thus, the *Jawz disc* was born.

tough-biting canines but not so hard as to pose a risk of injury to canine teeth. The project took more than a year of hard work. Countless material formulations were sampled with results that failed to meet the high standards that we set for the project. Still we pressed on. Finally, we narrowed in on a polymer

LINK To view a video of the *Jawz disc* being tested go to: http://hyperflite.com/jawzdiscs.html

It's no exaggeration to say that the *Jawz disc* represents the most significant

Hyperflite Comes to the Rescue! A zookeeper in the reptile house of the Metropolitan Zoo in Testudo, California contacted Hyperflite to inquire about a rush order of the incredibly tough Jawz canine disc. The zookeeper explained that the Zoo's beloved Himalayan Barking Tortoise, named "Sparky," had been injured by a groundskeeper in a freak weed-whacker incident. "Sparky" had a gaping hole

in the top of his shell that was drawing the attention of other zoo animals, in particular, the Portuguese prong-beaked storks, a breed known for their fondness of turtle meat. The powerful and razor sharp beak of the prong-beaked stork is capable of cracking tough mussel shells with aplomb.

"Sparky" needed immediate protection while his shell healed. The zookeeper had heard from his dog-owning neighbor about the incredibly tough and puncture-resistant Jawz disc. With the Jawz disc epoxied to his shell, "Sparky" can now crawl among the Storks with impunity. Hyperflite is committed to making the toughest and best-flying canine discs on the planet. Do your dog a favor and shell out a few dollars for the best-flying canine disc ever made.

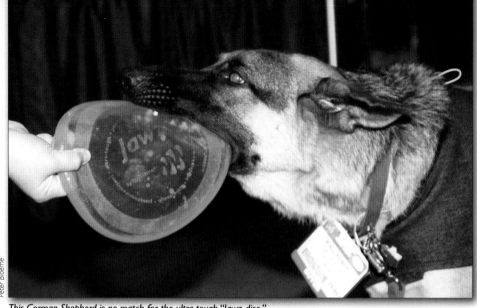

This German Shepherd is no match for the ultra-tough "Jawz disc."

Not surprisingly the "Jawz disc" will withstand the dreaded pink Poodle and the ferocious sweatered Dachshund.

technological development in the history of canine disc sports. The *Jawz* means that, for a new generation of competitors, participation in the sport will be a lot more affordable. On the day we announced the *Jawz*, we declared that *the days of gnash it and trash it* are finally over. The *Jawz* was an overnight sensation, and in high demand from the start. We could have let it go at that but there was still work to be done.

Next, we set about developing polymer formulations to address the needs of other groups of canine disc aficionados whose needs had been ignored for more than 30 years. In rapid succession,

Hyperflite FrostBite Disc

Peter Bloeme

Peter Bloeme

Hyperflite believes in thorough product testing for all of its products.

Hyperflite SofFlite Disc

we developed the *FrostBite* — a disc that remains flexible in cold weather and doesn't become brittle and shatter; and the *SofFlite* — a soft and flexible disc for puppies and older canines with sensitive mouths.

LINK To view a video of the *FrostBite* disc go to: http://hyperflite.com/frostbitediscs.html

LINK To view a video of the *SofFlite* disc go to: http://hyperflite.com/sofflitediscs.html

Hyperflite then looked to remedy an inequity that had always existed in canine disc sports — namely, that small dogs were forced to compete against larger canines using large discs that put them at a competitive disadvantage. To level the playing field, Hyperflite created a smaller but still great-flying version of the *K-10* disc and named it the *K-10 Pup. Pup discs* are one-third smaller than the legendary *K-10* and much easier for smaller dogs to catch and carry. Hyperflite's *Pup* discs are the official discs of the MicroDog Division of the Skyhoundz World Championship.

PRO TIP *I always keep a supply of discs in several colors available. Because my dogs are tough biters, I use black "Jawz X-Comp discs" against a hazy sky or when green trees are in the background. I use lemon-lime or tangerine "Jawz discs" against a deep blue sky. My rule of thumb is always contrast before color. In other words, the color matters less than the contrast created against the background.*
— *Jeff Stanaway, 2003 Hyperflite Skyhoundz World Champion*

Hyperflite Competition Standard Disc

Hyperflite Midnight Sun Disc

Hyperflite UV Disc

To view information about *Competition Standard* discs go to: http://hyperflite.com/competitionstandarddiscs.html

To view information on the *Midnight Sun* disc (glow-in-the-dark) go to: http://hyperflite.com/midnightsundisc.html

To view information on the *UV* disc (color changing) go to: http://hyperflite.com/uvdisc.html

In October of 2005, we received notice that Hyperflite had been awarded a U.S. Patent (Patent No. 6,887,119) for the *K-10's* improved flying disc design. The patent was the first patent ever granted for a disc specifically designed for canine competition.

Despite Hyperflite's sponsorship of the Skyhoundz World Canine Disc Championship Series, we believe that disc choice is a fundamental right of every disc dogger, and this is a right we honor at all Hyperflite-sponsored contests. Free disc choice, we maintain, encourages innovation among manufacturers. This truth has been borne out by recent disc introductions from manufacturers whose canine disc offerings have remained stagnant for decades. It is not coincidence, but rather, competition that has forced change.

In the end, the disc you choose will be determined by the temperament of your canine, the prevailing conditions, the preferences of you and your canine, and the task at hand. You may choose a soft and flexible disc like the *SofFlite* for a new puppy or an older dog. Or, you may opt for a *Jawz* disc for your toothy *Laughing Hyena* hybrid. Some competitors prefer lightweight discs like the Hyperflite *Competition Standard*. No matter which disc you choose, it's good that you finally have a choice.

DISC COLOR

Canines were once thought to be color blind; that is, that they could see only black and white and shades of gray. Canine eyes, like human eyes, contain within their retinas, certain light sensitive cells called cones and rods. Cones allow us to see small details as well as colors while rods allow us to detect motion and to see well in low-light conditions. Canine eyes have rod-dominated retinas and possess only about 10% of the cones that human eyes have. But don't let all this talk about cones and rods confuse you. All you really need to know is that dogs see great in low-light situations but can't see colors as well as humans can.

Modern studies on canine eyesight generally agree that dogs:

- Have eyes that allow for the optimal tracking of objects in motion.
- Have excellent night or low-light vision.
- Have limited or less-developed color vision.
- Have less developed close-up vision.

The colors that canines are believed to see well include: blue, purple, red, and yellow. However, canine vision depends upon so many variables, including ambient light, background, motion and even the shade of a particular color, that the proper disc to use in a given situation should best be determined after careful consideration of all of these factors and perhaps after a few test throws to your canine.

Generally speaking, if you wish to maximize the visibility of a disc to your canine then you must seek a disc that is clearly distinguishable from background clutter by virtue of the contrast that it

Jeremy Angel

Dogs enjoy playing in the snow. Be sure to examine their paw pads periodically for signs of injury or wear.

presents against the background in question. In making your disc selection, beware of the *amphitheater effect* that can occur when opposite ends of a playing field have very different backgrounds. For instance, a throw in one direction might be against a milky-white overcast while a throw in the opposite direction might yield a background of green trees or brown mountains. Polar-opposite backgrounds that occur at the same competition venue should cause you to select a compromise disc color that will be viewable by your canine against both backgrounds. And just to make things a little more complicated for you, research has also shown that the color green appears to canines to be yellow. So, even though dogs see yellow as yellow, and see the color yellow well, they also see green as yellow. A yellow disc against a background of green trees in certain light conditions might be difficult

for your canine to track. The only way to be sure that your canine can see a particular disc well would be to make a few practice throws to confirm that the disc can easily be seen by your canine under the conditions present.

Also, since conditions change during the course of a day, the disc you choose in the morning, may not be the same disc that you should use in the afternoon.

Interestingly, the results from one of the key studies done on the interpretation of color by canines don't always correlate with the experiences of many disc doggers who swear by one disc color or another. These disparities suggest that between and among breeds, and even from canine-to-canine, dogs may not *see* eye-to-eye.

Disc Gimmicks

Once you begin to train your dog with a canine competition disc, you will quickly learn that all of the gimmicks such as

Peter Bloeme

We got in trouble for this one!

2004 World Finalist "Gretchen" making a
great effort in Distance/Accuracy.

rubber discs, whistling discs, discs with battery-powered lights, discs with protruding features, flavored discs, etc., simply can't hold a candle to a modern competition disc designed with superior aerodynamics and lightweight super-strong polymers. Rubber discs, for example, may make fine fetch toys, but, because of their weight, they don't fly well and you simply won't see them in competition. Inexpensive promotional discs made of hard plastic can shatter and cause injury. Choose only safe flying discs form a reputable manufacturer.

There are many flying disc gimmicks on the market; some are even specifically geared toward dog owners. They may be great for adult play and collecting, but generally we recommend that you stick with reliable and safe competition-approved discs for your dog.

Sven Van Driessche

Ouch...that smarts!

LINK Visit the Hyperflite website at http://hyperflite.com for more information on Hyperflite canine discs.

Disc Maintenance

You will probably notice that with play, certain discs will develop rough and sharp edges. If you leave them that way

Thom Gillott

Fabric discs don't fly that well and generally aren't approved for competition.

Does your dog need a Jawz disc?

Disc Aerodynamics

A flying disc operates in accordance with the same scientific principles that govern any other airfoil, meaning it is designed to produce a reaction from the air. The concept is simple. The air that passes over the disc travels faster than the air passing underneath the disc. The air movement around the disc causes a low-pressure area to develop on top of the disc and a high-pressure area to develop below the disc. The combination of the two pressures on the top and bottom of the disc causes the disc's rotating airfoil to generate lift.

The rotation of a disc in flight, contrary to popular belief, does not contribute to lift but rather, adds stability. The faster you make a disc spin, the more stable it will be. A disc that wobbles probably doesn't have enough spin. Try pushing a disc through the air with no spin. You'll find that it flutters and falls.

The combination of good arm speed, a smooth release, and a strong spin-generating wrist snap, will create the conditions necessary for optimal disc flight. These techniques can be mastered by anyone, with practice, and are described more thoroughly in the chapter that follows.

they can cut your dog's mouth or tongue. The remedy is simple: trim any protrusions or nicks and, with fine-grade sandpaper, file any remaining rough spots down. Proper disc maintenance will extend the life of your discs and save you money. Also, between practice sessions, be sure to wipe off the discs so that there is no dirt, saliva, or grit left on them.

A dishwasher works great for cleaning discs though you may want to deselect the dry cycle or you may warp your discs.

Grit and dirt can act like revolving sandpaper on canine teeth. Hyperflite discs were designed with ultra-low profile grip surfaces that do not trap and retain grit and dirt like most other discs marketed to canine disc enthusiasts. Regardless of the type of disc you use, cleaning your discs after play or practice sessions will help keep them more sanitary and consequently safer for your dog.

Flying discs like the Jawz disc are designed to hold up to the toughest of biters and they don't generally require much care and maintenance. They are not, however, intended to be canine chew toys. As long as you remember not to leave Jawz discs with your dog when your play session is finished, they can last an unbelievably long time.

2005 Open Division World Champions Tony Hoard and "Rory."

Throwing
Chapter 7

For many, throwing a disc well is the most difficult aspect of canine disc training. However, it is technique, rather than strength, that marks the best throwers. Although developing the proper technique comes quite naturally to some, others have to work diligently to get the hang of it. Like many other things in life, you get out of it, what you put into it. If you don't practice consistently in a variety of conditions you and your canine will be, quite literally, at the mercy of the wind.

In order to throw a disc well you must do the following:

- Maintain a proper grip on the disc
- Use the proper throwing stance
- Make use of your entire body during the throwing motion as opposed to just your arm and wrist.
- Impart sufficient spin to the disc during the throwing motion to provide stability to the disc in flight
- Release the disc at the proper angle for the prevailing conditions

When starting out, make short throws to a partner or to a fixed tar-

On the other end of most good catches is a good throw.

Peter Bloeme

If you make good throws, your dog has a better chance of catching them.

get on a fence or other barrier. As your accuracy improves, you can move further from your target. Trying to throw far without adequate control over the trajectory of your discs puts your canine at risk and will ingrain bad habits that will be difficult to overcome in the future. Only after you have control over the disc should you attempt to throw to your canine.

When starting out, the most important thing to remember is to keep the disc's flight as flat as possible. Flying discs released with a bank angle (more properly referred to as *hyzer*), tend to turn in the direction of the bank angle. Throws made with the disc leading edge pitched up or down, will climb or descend, respectively.

> **PRO TIP**
>
> *The Eyes Have It — You may have the perfect music, tricks, throws, and canine, but the sum of all those components may not be what it should be. Sometimes an extra set of eyes on the sidelines can give you a few pointers in order to make it all flow. Invite your family or a few close friends for dinner and, for dessert, give them a high-flying disc dog show. Then, while you've got them where you want them, ask for their impressions of your performance. Specifically, what areas of the routine looked slow, rushed, or just didn't work at all. They might even have a few suggestions for new tricks that you can add to your routine. When friends and family are scarce then how about a digital friend? Reviewing a videotape can provide an excellent opportunity for you to critique your own routine.*
>
> *— Shannon Bilheimer, 2005-2007 Hyperflite Skyhoundz*
> *Pairs Freestyle World Champion*

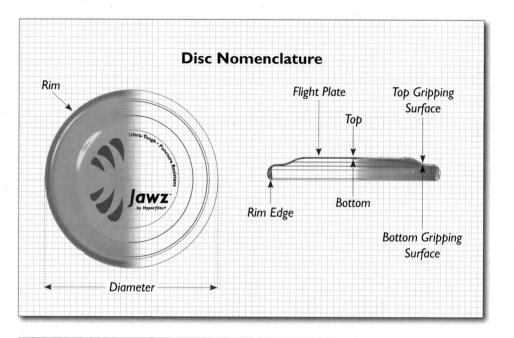

Disc Nomenclature

Rim

Flight Plate

Top Gripping Surface

Top

Rim Edge

Bottom

Bottom Gripping Surface

Diameter

Ultra-Tough • Puncture Resistant

Jawz™
by Hyperflite®

Although it is sometimes difficult to visualize the throwing motion through written descriptions or photographs, all is not lost. If you still can't grasp the mechanics after reviewing the descriptions, photos and diagrams that follow, consider picking up a copy of Hyperflite's *Disc Dog Training DVD* or the classic *Disc Dogs Throwing Video/DVD*. When you see the throwing motion in slow-motion video, it is usually a light-bulb experience for most folks.

LINK *Disc Dog Training DVD* and *Disc Dog Throwing Video/DVD* are available at the Skyhoundz store www.skyhoundz.com

GRIP

Use a firm but not tight grip to hold the disc. After you develop a comfortable grip, practice it repeatedly until it becomes second nature. As in golf and tennis, a good grip is paramount to success.

SPIN

Always put a generous amount of spin on the disc upon release. The more spin, the longer the disc will maintain its stability. At first, beginners can simply concentrate on wrist snap. Ideally, however, spin is imparted to a disc through several factors, including proper body position and a snapping motion that originates from a steady stance and progresses through the hips, arm, elbow and, finally, the wrist.

STANCE

The proper stance for the backhand throw, the most versatile throw for disc dog play, requires that you stand sideways to your intended target with your feet a shoulders' width apart and your knees slightly bent and parallel to each other. Start the throwing motion with two-thirds of your weight on your back foot. Then shift it naturally forward to

A nice grab!

Jeff Percy

your front foot (leaving one-third of your weight on your back foot) as you release the disc. Try not to lift your back foot off the ground and lunge forward as you throw. If you do, you will have difficulty controlling your tosses. Your stance will, of course, be different for each throw but keep in mind that a stable platform will help you make stable throws.

HYZER AND ANHYZER

Perhaps the single most difficult concept for novice disc doggers to master is the concept of *hyzer*. The name *hyzer* probably arose from the *Hi Sir* greeting typically extended to expert disc tossers in the late 1800's although the true origin of the term is still in dispute. In disc dog sports, *hyzer* refers to the bank angle of the disc at the point of release. Once you understand how *hyzer* impacts the flight of the disc and begin to make practical use of varied bank angles when you throw, it will be smooth sailing for you and your canine.

While it may appear to the casual observer that most throwers release their discs with a flat trajectory, this is not the case. The best throwers understand the aerodynamics associated with disc flight and they know that as a disc slows down, and loses its rotational stability, it will slowly begin to turn in the direction that the disc is spinning. For a right-handed thrower making a standard backhand delivery, as the disc slows down, it will begin to curve or break to the right. To counteract this tendency, a good thrower will add *hyzer* (increased bank angle in the opposite direction) to the throw. Ideally, you want the disc to finish its flight in a level attitude so that your canine can make an easy catch.

The bank angle at release is determined by a number of factors in-

Keep both feet on the ground for consistent throws.

cluding the type of disc you are using, whether the disc has surface imperfections (tooth marks or holes) that cause drag, the distance you are attempting to throw, and, most importantly, the velocity of the wind that you are throwing into. Here are some general rules that will help you get the big picture of how to use *hyzer* to your advantage.

- Older-style discs like the *Fastback disc* from Wham-O are not as aerodynamic as more modern designs like the Competition Standard *disc*. To keep *Fastback discs* from turning over as they fly, you will need to use a lot more *hyzer*.

- If you are throwing into a strong wind, you may need an extreme, nearly vertical bank angle in order to keep a disc from rolling rapidly to the right. Whereas, if you are throwing with the wind at your back, a flat release will probably suffice.

- Crosswind throws may necessitate a flat release to keep tosses from sailing off the playing field.

- If you are making a very long throw, then the disc will be moving pretty fast through the air. As a rule, long throws require more *hyzer* than short throws.

- Discs in perfect condition will fly differently than worn discs. Parasite drag caused by superficial damage (tooth marks or holes) to your discs will increase the amount of *hyzer* required to keep a worn disc from over rotating as it flies. That is why it is not a good idea to switch to brand new discs right before a competition without first practicing with them. Don't forget that it's the little things that can ruin your day on the field of competition.

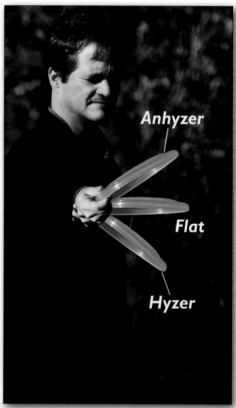

Examples of "anhyzer," "flat," and "hyzer" release angles. (You'd close your eyes too if your knuckles looked like this!)

"Catch that for me, won't you 'Chauncy?'"

Professionals at work.

Finally, you should also know that *hyzer* has a sister throw referred to as *anhyzer*. *Anhyzer* is simply bank angle that will cause a disc thrown by a right hand thrower (using the backhand grip) to curve to the right. It is used in throws like the upside-down throw described later in this chapter. Whether you use *hyzer* or *anhyzer* to make a throw to your canine will depend upon how you want the disc to fly after you release it. When you finally understand the interrelationship between the two *hyzer siblings*, you will be ready to develop your own trick throws and handle windy days like a professional.

Sven Van Driessche

GRAVY

Theresa Musi, of Atlanta, Georgia, and her canine pal "Ciela Azule," are veteran disc dog competitors. But the challenges that "Ciela" faces are quite different from most other disc dogs. In addition to her disc dog duties, "Ciela" is also Musi's service dog.

Even while competing, "Ciela" must keep a watchful eye on Musi looking for the subtle signs, that only certain canines can detect, that warn of the onset of seizures. Musi has experienced periodic epileptic seizures since she was 4 years old. Before "Ciela," Musi's world was always plagued by uncertainty. "I never knew when the seizures would come and that made it more challenging to enjoy many activities," Musi laments. But with "Ciela," things are very different. "What 'Ciela' does for me," Musi says, "is give me enough time to be somewhere safe when the seizures hit — so I can workout, drive a car, hike or do anything else I want to do without worry." "Because of 'Ciela,'" Musi adds, "I feel normal for the first time in my life."

— *Theresa Musi, 2004-2006 Hyperflite Skyhoundz World Finalist*

Kendall Lemley and "Johnny!"

THROWS

BACKHAND THROW

The backhand throw is a versatile and easy-to-learn delivery. Once mastered, it can be used for accuracy, distance and trick throws.

We recommend a combination of popular grips called the *Modified Berkeley Power Grip*. Make a fist with your palm up and open your thumb to the hitchhiking position. Loosen your fingers just enough to slip the disc between your palm and finger tips and place your thumb on the top grip surface of the disc. Now, bring your other hand up and hold the other side of the disc temporarily. Move the fingers of your gripping hand slightly toward your thumb (while trying to maintain as much contact as possible with the inside rim) until they feel somewhat comfortable. For shorter throws, you can move the tips of your two middle fingers onto the underside grip surface of the disc.

Do not place your index finger along the outside rim of the disc, since doing so will cause you to lose accuracy, power and control. Maintain a firm grip by

Backhand Grip: Side View

squeezing the disc between your palm and the last two fingers (pinkie and ring finger) of your hand. This will allow you to snap the throw. It may seem like a subtle change but it can really affect your throwing.

If you are right handed, stand sideways to your target with your right foot forward. Bring the disc back across your body to just above your left side until your arm is as far back as your left shoulder. Your arm should be bent

Sven Van Driessche (Sequence)

Jeff Perry using the backhand grip for a between-the-legs underhand throw to "K.D."

Backhand Grip: Top View

Backhand Grip: Bottom View

slightly, with your wrist bent inward and the disc held flat.

The throwing motion should be left to right, smooth and even, with a good snap upon release. Do not rotate your wrist from side to side, only forward and backward as if you were doing wrist curls with a dumbbell. As you make the throw, follow through with your right hand extended toward the target as you might if you were reaching out to shake someone's hand. Keep your eyes on your intended target as you make your throws. If your throws go to the left of the target you're releasing the disc too soon. If your throws veer to the right, then you are releasing the disc too late. Most right-handed throwers fall into the too-late category and hook their throws to the right. If your throws wobble in flight, then try to concentrate on a nice smooth wrist snap as you release the disc.

Frame 1 Backhand Sequence: Body position perpendicular to the direction you are throwing. Your feet a shoulder-width apart, knees slightly bent., head forward.

Frame 2 Backhand Sequence: Weight should shift slightly forward. Keep eyes on target, stay relaxed.

Frame 3 Backhand Sequence: You don't need a long follow through. For short distance throws try to stop your arm with your hand pointing at the target.

ROLLER THROW

The roller throw is commonly used to train a beginning disc dog or puppy. Roller throws are easy and fun for dogs to track. To make a roller toss, use the backhand grip. The release angle for a roller is steep, almost vertical. Kneel or squat down and bring your throwing hand to your chest. With the disc laying flat on your chest, snap your wrist forward and down. If you released the disc perpendicular to the ground it should roll along nicely on the outside of the rim until your eager canine grabs it.

Roller throws, although seemingly simple, can be jazzed up and incorporated into advanced disc dog routines. Experiment with interesting roller throw deliveries. Perhaps you can make a roller toss using your feet. Or, try putting backspin on the disc to cause it to roll between your legs with your canine in hot pursuit. You can roll a disc along your back and have your canine catch it before it hits the ground. The roller toss

Roller Grip: Side View

always makes us think of the good old days before innovation sent the roller to its competitive grave. It is always nice to see old tricks, like the roller, rejuvenated in an interesting or innovative way. Here is a description of a trick that we have always wanted to see. It's called Boomerang Multiples. To do this trick, make a curving roller toss that will ultimately

Sven Van Driessche (Sequence)

Hyperflite Skyhoundz World Finalist Timmie Dohn makes a roller throw to her dog "Dakota."

Roller Grip: Top View

Roller Grip: Bottom View

find its way back to you. As your canine begins to pursue the roller, make several successive throws to your dog in such a way as to allow him to catch your tosses while continuing in a circle that follows the path of the roller toss. Then, before the roller makes it all the way back to you, have your canine grab it to complete the trick sequence. This trick would showcase a canine's ability to move quickly between multiple throws while maintaining focus on the ultimate prize…the roller.

"Troyca" locks-on to the target.

Sven Van Driessche

Frame 1 Roller Sequence: Your front knee should be down, so you don't bump it with the disc, or your arm, as you throw.

Frame 2 Roller Sequence: The throwing motion is brisk.

Frame 3 Roller Sequence: Finish with a good wrist snap.

UPSIDE-DOWN SLIDER THROW

This is also an excellent throw for training a new puppy and is also best thrown from a kneeling position. To make an upside-down slider throw, grip the disc as shown here. Basically, the upside-down slider grip is a mirror image of the backhand grip...simply hold an inverted disc as if it were right side up. Your grip pressure should be between your thumb (which is pressed against the inside rim of the disc), and your first finger. You may have to adjust your fingers slightly to get comfortable. Instead of releasing the disc high in the air, throw it flat parallel to, and just barely above, the ground so that it skips or slides like a hockey puck. This throw can be used indoors with great success.

Upside-down slider throws are very versatile and can be made from behind your back, in multiple sequences, or

Upside-Down Slider Grip: Side View

even between your legs. If your puppy has trouble picking the disc off of the ground when the disc lands right side up, inverted tosses are a great way to keep him from becoming frustrated and losing interest.

Frame 1 Upside-Down Slider Sequence: As with most throws a good snap is key.

Frame 2 Upside-Down Slider Sequence: Release the disc at, or below, shoulder height.

Upside-Down Slider Grip: Top View

Upside-Down Slider Grip: Bottom View

When training a new puppy you can use the upside-down slider as part of a keep-away game to get your pup interested in the disc. With a friend positioned 10 feet away, simply slide or bat an inverted disc back and forth across the ground or a carpeted surface. Act as if you're having a grand-old-time and soon your young trainee will want to participate in the fun!

Frame 3 Upside-Down Slider Sequence: Because inverted throws are flying upside-down, they fall quickly to the ground and can slide for some distance.

INVERTED OR UPSIDE-DOWN THROW

The upside-down throw can be made with a variety of deliveries and is a nice change of pace for canines used to catching discs that are almost always right-side up. Making and catching an upside-down toss can be more challenging because flying discs, like most asymmetrical airfoils, do not fly well when they are inverted. Accordingly, some adjustment to your throwing technique will be required in order to keep a disc thrown with an inverted throw in the air long enough for your canine to catch. The inverted backhand throw is one of the easiest upside-down throws to make. To make this throw you grip the disc as you would for an up-side-down slider throw. Use the same *sideways-to-the-target* stance as used for the backhand throw. Instead of bringing your throwing arm across your body

Upside-Down Grip: Side View

in a parallel motion as you do with the backhand throw, you start the disc at shoulder level and release the disc up, and out, with a gentle looping trajectory. If released flat, the disc will tend to quickly over rotate and fall to earth. Therefore, the perfect inverted back-

Frame 1 Upside-Down Sequence: Your weight should shift slightly forward as the throw progresses.

Frame 2 Upside-Down Sequence: Very little twisting of the hips is required for this throw.

Upside-Down Grip: Top View

Upside-Down Grip: Bottom View

hand throw should be released with a 15 to 45° bank angle depending upon the length of the throw, the condition of the disc and the velocity of the wind.

This throw is a shoulder-arm-wrist throw that requires minimal twisting of the torso...great for folks with bad backs.

Frame 3 Upside-Down Sequence: The release is generally over your head with significant "anhyzer."

Frame 4 Upside-Down Sequence: A well thrown upside-down toss follows a high and curving trajectory to the target.

ADVANCED THROWS

Since the calibre of competition has grown tremendously in recent years, it is helpful to learn some advanced throws now commonly used in canine disc play. Even if you decide not to compete, they are still fun for your dog to catch and they will make you look like a superstar at your local park.

SIDEARM THROW

The sidearm throw is an advanced, but common throw, in which only three fingers are used to grip the disc. To make the sidearm throw, turn the disc upside-down. Make a peace or victory sign with your index and middle finger. Place your middle finger against the inside rim of the disc while keeping your index finger flat against the flight plate. Grip the top of the disc with your thumb. Now turn the disc right-side-up. Your last two fingers are bent and used as a guide. With the proper grip, stand sideways to your target and bend your arm at a 90° angle while keep-

Sidearm Grip: Side View

ing your elbow close to your body. Flex your wrist back and then snap it forward. Concentrate on using mostly wrist action rather than arm motion for this throw.

The best use of the basic sidearm throw that we have seen was by 1991 World Champion Ron Ellis with his dog *Maggy*. He had a four-throw combina-

Jeff Stanaway demonstrates a blind sidearm throw, while his dog "Cory" races between his legs and makes a jumping catch.

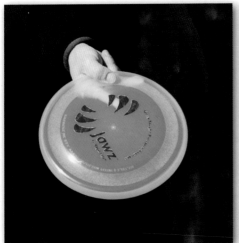

Sidearm Grip: Top View

Sidearm Grip: Bottom View

tion series that included some really beautiful and rock-solid sidearm throws. Jeff Gabel, a two-time world champion, used an advanced version of the sidearm throw with great success. He would run toward his dog *Casey*, as *Casey* ran toward him. As the two were about to collide, Gabel would leap over his dog while simultaneously making a blind between-the-legs sidearm toss to *Casey* who continued in the opposite direction to make the catch. *Casey* really seemed to kick in the afterburners to catch Gabel's unique sidearm delivery.

Frame 1 Sidearm Sequence: Use less arm motion and more wrist snap with this throw.

Frame 2 Sidearm Sequence: Twist your hips, waist, and torso for extra distance.

Frame 3 Sidearm Sequence: Finish with a strong snap.

OVERHAND WRIST-FLIP

The overhand wrist-flip is a cool-looking throw that most people pick up quite easily. To make the overhand wrist-flip, imagine that you are holding the disc in your throwing hand as if it were a dinner plate. Now turn that dinner plate (disc) upside down. Extend your throwing arm and raise it to shoulder level as you would if you were holding your arms out at your sides. Now, you should be holding the disc right-side-up and on a plane level with your shoulder. While maintaining the disc on a level plane, reach back as far as you can with your arm (you might want to twist your hips), then quickly move your arm forward and release the disc with a good wrist snap. As you release the disc, it will feel as if you are trying to put backspin on the disc, and indeed, an inverted wrist-flip throw does cause the disc to spin in the opposite direction of a backhand throw.

The overhand wrist-flip looks great when used in a multiple series with other

Overhand Wrist-Flip Grip: Side View

interesting throws. If you really want to impress the judges, try making an *inverted* overhand wrist-flip throw. To make the inverted version of the overhand wrist-flip, the throwing motion is the same but the disc is held inverted using the standard backhand grip. The delivery will feel a bit awkward but once you master it, it is

Sven Van Driessche (Sequence)

2005 Hyperflite Skyhoundz World Champion Tony Hoard makes an overhand wrist-flip throw to his dog, "Rory," who runs

Overhand Wrist-Flip Grip: Top View

Overhand Wrist-Flip Grip: Bottom View

an impressive throw. By the way, the inverted version of the overhand wrist-flip is not a throw that should be attempted by those with shoulder or elbow problems. Also, the bank angle (*hyzer/anhyzer*) of the disc at release will be critical. Nail this throw, and you may even amaze your own canine!

between his legs before making the catch.

Frame 1 Overhand Wrist-Flip Sequence: Curl your wrist so that the disc is touching or close to your forearm.

Frame 2 Overhand Wrist-Flip Sequence: Twist your body as you swing your arm forward.

Frame 3 Overhand Wrist-Flip Sequence: Finish with a good sharp wrist snap.

BUTTERFLY

Flying discs are most commonly thrown vertically, horizontally, or upside down. Although a disc flies best when it is spinning, there are other interesting ways to deliver a disc to your eager canine. One of those deliveries is commonly called the butterfly throw — though it is also known as an end-over-end toss or third-world spin. A butterfly toss, in flight, looks exactly like the classic heads or tails coin toss. It tumbles rather than spins. Over the years, competitors have come up with myriad variations of butterfly throws and, because of their apparent difficulty, many competitors incorporate at least one butterfly into their routines. Again, there are at least fourteen gazillion variations of this throw and, chances are, you can come up with one of your own!

The basic butterfly toss is made like this: first, from a standing position, hold a disc, upside down, in the palm of your

Butterfly Grip: Side View

throwing hand, as if you were holding a dinner plate while working your way through the chow line. The rim of the disc should not rest deeply in your palm but should, instead, fall approximately where your fingers join your hand. To make a butterfly toss, simply make a rapid downward snapping motion that causes the

Butterfly Sequence: A disc that rotates too quickly or too slowly will be difficult for your canine to catch.

Sven Van Driessche (Sequence)

Butterfly Grip: Top View

Butterfly Grip: Bottom View

disc to tumble end-over-end as it leaves your hand. It may take a while to develop the coordination and wrist strength to get a good snapping motion down pat but keep at it and it will eventually come naturally to you. The butterfly tumbling motion of the disc can also be induced with a two handed throw, by a tap with a free hand, or by a kick with your foot. With a little effort and ingenuity, you will undoubtedly amaze the competition judges with your own take on this classic throw.

Frame 1 Butterfly Sequence: Accelerate your arm rapidly as you begin this throw.

Frame 2 Butterfly Sequence: As your arm extends begin to uncurl your wrist.

Frame 3 Butterfly Sequence: Abruptly stop your arm motion and release the disc when your arm is almost extended.

Frame 4 Butterfly Sequence: Snap it hard yet smoothly or the disc will wobble.

TWO-HANDED PUSH TOSS

This is an excellent short-distance throw that is seldom used in competition though it would be excellent for adding a bit of variety into a freestyle routine. Two-handed throws give you tremendous control over the disc's angle of attack because the throw starts right in front of your face so it's easy to see your mistakes.

Explaining this throw in words is considerably more difficult than actually making the throw (see photos here) — but here goes. Place your hands together so they are touching, in a prayer-type position, with the tips of your fingers pointed up and at your eye level. Open your hands wide enough to firmly hold a disc between your hands. The disc should be level as if hovering in front of your face and the sides of the disc should rest on the second finger joint of both hands. Without letting go

Two-Handed Grip: Side View

of the disc, bring it close to your face so that it nearly touches your nose. Keep the disc level as you quickly push it away from your face while simultaneously rotating and releasing the disc with your hands. It looks a bit like you are making

2007 Hyperflite Skyhoundz World Champion Danny Venegas demonstrates a two-handed push toss to an "over."

Two-Handed Grip: Top View

Two-Handed Grip: Bottom View

simultaneous karate chops with your hands, one away from, and the other toward your face. The rapid opposing karate chop motion of your hands imparts a stabilizing spinning force on the disc. Once you perfect the basic form of the two-handed toss you can hold your hands over your head and make the same toss. For even more difficulty you can lean back and make the throw behind you.

Frame 1 Two-Handed Sequence: Push tosses are great fun for canines.

Frame 2 Two-Handed Sequence: A Push toss can be made straight up or in any direction desired.

Frame 3 Two-Handed Sequence: A smooth release will keep your push toss level.

Frame 4 Two-Handed Sequence: Again, it's all about the spin!

THUMB THROW

The thumb throw, or thumber as it is often called, is an easy throw to make though it can be difficult to achieve mastery over the directional control of discs thrown with this technique. To throw a thumber, use the same grip that is used for the upside down slider throw and merely turn your wrist over and lay the disc on top of your forearm. Stand sideways to your target and draw your arm back in the ready position. With the disc still laying level on your forearm, rapidly twist your torso and upper body and release the disc with a good snap. The disc will fairly fly off your thumb as you finish the throw square to (facing) your intended target. Thumbers can also be made inverted using a grip that pinches the leading edge of the disc between

Thumb Throw Grip: Side View

your thumb and curled (like your making a fist) index finger. This type of inverted throw, although technically a thumber, will feel almost like an inverted sidearm

Frame 1 Thumb Throw Sequence: Lay the disc on your forearm as you begin the throwing motion.

Frame 2 Thumb Throw Sequence: A good twisting motion that starts with your waist will generate lots of energy.

Thumb Throw Grip: Top View

Thumb Throw Grip: Bottom View

throw. For a right-handed thrower, a thumber will spin vigorously in the opposite direction of a backhand throw. Make sure your canine sees you as you make this throw, otherwise he'll have no way of anticipating this rapidly spinning disc. In competition, the thumber is but another arrow in your quiver.

Frame 3 Thumb Throw Sequence: Your body will be "square" to your target at the point of release.

Frame 4 Thumb Throw Sequence: The disc flies off your thumb earning its thumber nickname.

AIRBRUSH

The airbrush is like getting two throws for the price of one. Of course, you have to *pay* a lot, in terms of practice, to earn the right to use the airbrush, for it is a challenging throw to master. Now, let's get back to the *two throws* thing.

First, an airbrush is really nothing more than a set-up throw that is redirected to a different flight path than the flight path that the disc originally embarked on. Still confused? OK, in the preferred embodiment — as a patent lawyer might say — an airbrush is made when a thrower makes a short toss to himself and, rather than catching the toss, he then redirects the disc by striking it obliquely with his hand or foot. The redirected toss (airbrush) is then caught by the canine. Sound easy? It's not. The airbrush is one of the more difficult throws to perfect. At first, novices typically make poor set-up throws, or miss-hit the disc, causing the attempted airbrush to wobble at best or, at worst, fall out of the air like a wounded duck.

To ensure success, be sure to put a lot of spin on your set-up toss. Then

Jeff Perry "sets up" Peter Bloeme with a two-handed push toss.

strike the disc edge, with a glancing blow, in the same direction that the disc is spinning. If you brush the disc with your foot, the outside edge of your foot works best. If done well, the airbrush is quite impressive and will undoubtedly make you look like a freestyle master in the eyes of the disc dog rabble.

Sven Van Driessche (Sequence)

Airbrushes can be made by slapping the rim of the disc with the palm of your hand or by kicking the rim of a spinning disc with

Sven Van Driessche (Sequence)

Bloeme then airbrushes the disc to "K.D."

Finally, a word of caution is in order. Practice the airbrush alone, until you have it mastered. When you finally attempt it with your canine present, have a helper restrain your dog so that he can get a feel for what you are attempting to do. You wouldn't want to accidently kick or whack your best buddy in the noggin' in your blind zeal to brush it like a pro.

the side of your foot.

SKIP

A skip occurs when a thrower causes a disc to bounce off the ground and back into the air. Skip throws are not particularly popular in competition because the skipping surface (usually grass) varies so much that it is difficult to perform skips predictably. Taller grass is more difficult to skip a disc from than short grass. Still, some people do use the skip in competition for variety as long as they have a suitable surface to work from. It is challenging for a beginner to learn a skip throw on all but the shortest grass, so practice skip throws on a firm dirt surface, such as a baseball infield, before trying them on grass. You can make skip throws off of concrete or asphalt surfaces, but you will damage your discs if you do. It goes without saying (even though we're saying it) that you should never play with your dog on concrete, asphalt or any other hard surface because of the possibility of injury.

To make a skip throw, use the backhand grip, but instead of releasing the

Skip Grip: Side View

disc in a level attitude, you throw it with the outside edge of the disc angled downward (i.e., a healthy portion of hyzer) at about a 45° angle to the ground. The outside edge of the disc (not the leading edge) should contact the ground slightly less than half-way to your intended target. Yes, that's right, it is the outside edge of the disc, rather than

Svin Van Driessche (Sequence)

Skips are child's play for accomplished throwers and a challenge for disc dogs.

Skip Grip: Top View

Skip Grip: Bottom View

the leading edge that should contact the ground. If the disc contacts the ground too close to the thrower it will lose momentum and fall to the ground short of the target. A skip throw that contacts the ground significantly more than half-way to the target may bog down in the grass or not skip high enough to be caught by your canine.

Skip throws need lots of spin and velocity in order to overcome their brief encounter with drag-inducing grass. After you have mastered skips on a hard surface, practice on the shortest grass you can find. Believe it or not, with proper technique, a skip throw can even be made with the disc upside-down!

Frame 1 Backhand Skip Sequence: Aim for a spot on the ground between one-third and halfway to your target.

Frame 2 Backhand Skip Sequence: Use a good snap and extra arm for best results.

Frame 3 Backhand Skip Sequence: Plan to skip the disc on its outside edge, with lots of spin, for success.

Coming in for a landing at the World Championship.

Jay-Majdow

Disc Dogs! Basics

Chapter 8

By now, you've been working hard on your throwing and you're starting to get the hang of it. Your older canine or puppy has a good foundation of basic obedience training and you're beginning to think that it might be time to teach your dog to catch a flying disc. We would be neglectful if we didn't extend to you this warning: **Canine disc play is addictive!**

Your dog, in all probability, will become hooked on the flying disc, and may show little interest in activities that it formerly found interesting. Your canine's obsession with plastic may cause you to drive or fly hundreds, if not thousands, of miles to attend disc dog extravaganzas and hobnob with other like-minded disc doggers. Your life may well change in ways you could never have imagined. Just ask some of the, doctors, lawyers, software engineers, teachers, secretaries, business owners, and people from all walks of life — even a few perfectly normal folks — who have been bitten by the disc dog bug.

Some of these people have gone so far as to give up their comfortable lifestyles to tour with the circus, start rescue organizations, or become veterinarians. It's impossible to tell how your disc dog experience will affect your life, but it most definitely will.

THE FIRST STEPS

If you've read this far, then you know that we have probably described five or more training tips or methods as *crucial* or *important*. Well, here's a new one. It's imperative that you keep your initial workout sessions short, possibly as short as a few throws. In the beginning, it is better to have multiple short sessions per day than one long session. Always stop before your dog gets tired

MicroDogs: More pounce per ounce!

or loses interest. Remember, you don't want your best friend to think that disc play is a chore! As with any canine training, make sure your canine is rewarded liberally with praise and that your training sessions are fun and relaxed. Since we will be working with our canines off leash, it is prudent to limit early disc dog training sessions to safe, fenced-in yards, parks, or other similar areas.

During the canine disc basic-training phase, it's a good idea to work on just one trick at a time so you don't confuse your pet. There will be plenty of time to put all of the tricks together into a routine as your dog's experience and enthusiasm levels increase.

Once your dog has mastered a trick, try a new one while continuing to practice and reinforce the old one. Every dog is different — some learn very quickly while others progress more slowly. Don't push your dog at too fast a pace or you and your canine may become discouraged.

As you progress, be observant and take note if your canine has certain natural tendencies or capabilities. The best disc doggers create tricks that take advantage of the strengths and natural tendencies of their canines. For instance, if your canine is super quick over short distances but slow on the long throws, then develop tricks and trick sequences

GRAVY

I was living with kidney disease and had been on dialysis for five years. The disease was taking a toll on me mentally and physically. I had become depressed and very afraid of dying. I've read many reports on how pets can comfort you during times of sickness and depression. Never owning a pet before, I thought, why not get a dog! So I did! I brought a four-pound Dachshund home and named him "Sammy Davis." At four months, and weighing only six pounds, "Sammy Davis" contracted parvo, a potentially life threatening disease. By this time I had become very attached to the little guy. I had to leave him with my vet, for treatment, for an entire week. When that long week was finally over I was able to take "Sammy Davis" home again. He had made a full recovery.

As I still was undergoing treatment myself, I would come home and rest. It seemed "Sammy Davis" would have none of me lying in bed all day. "Sammy Davis"'healing methods were simple and ultimately satisfying to both of us. He would repetitiously put into my hands toys, pieces of paper, or anything he thought would fly in the air, so that he could catch and retrieve. I began to think that this dog was telling me something. "Get up and live, its not over," "Sammy Davis" was letting me know. "You saved me, now its time I repay the favor."

Playing with "Sammy Davis" became a diversion that kept me from focusing on the difficult days I was used to in the past. I started to get up after treatment and feel like my life wasn't so dismal after all. After several months of catch I decided to introduce a flying disc to "Sammy Davis." He loved it! People are amazed to see that a Dachshund can run and jump and participate in disc dog activities. "Sammy Davis" gave me a sense of hope and brought out a spiritual side of me I never knew, and introduced me to a sport I never knew anything about. It's more than just a story. It's a miracle.

— Patrick Major, Disc Doggs of the Golden Gate

Sven Van Driessche

I'm done looking cute...can we play now?

getting angry as you train your canine, then stop disc training and play with a ball or other toy until you calm down. Dogs are incredibly sensitive creatures and if disc training seems to upset you, then no matter how much they enjoy it — they will balk or refuse to play. Once more for emphasis — keep it light and fun for your canine and your canine disc training will be a breeze.

As with obedience training, until your dog is 3 or 4 months old just let him be a puppy without a care in the world. In fact, you may want to wait until that age before getting a dog, since puppies need time with their mother and siblings for proper socialization and development. At three to four months of age, you can introduce your puppy to the disc by feeding and watering him from it. This works great for older dogs as well. You might also make short roller throws in a safe, fenced grassy area or indoors on a carpeted surface. If your dog chases, follows or grabs the disc, then be animated and liberal in your praise.

that emphasize quickness while avoiding the longer tosses.

Just as parents are sometimes overly ambitious with respect to their children, some disc dog trainers are a bit too eager with their canine disc training. Over the years we have seen quite a few talented disc dog candidates ruined by overly intense or bad-tempered trainers. If you find yourself

At six months you can begin disc dog training in earnest. There are some in the disc dog community and in the veterinary medicine field who believe that puppies should not be allowed to engage in canine disc play or any other vigorous activity until their growth plates close, which usually occurs around the time they are 18 months old. Some

How dogs fly!

Peter Bloeme

The quicker I eat, the sooner I get to play with it.

to burn off energy and properly develop muscles and coordination as they grow. Disc play is no more hazardous than any other activity that puppies will engage in as long as you follow some reasonable precautions. In fact, disc play is as safe, if not safer, than most unscripted and unsupervised activities that your puppy is likely to want to pursue. There are a few common sense precautions that you should take when training your younger canine. First, never attempt to teach your puppy or young canine *vaulting* tricks. *Vaulting*, when a canine jumps off a trainers leg, back, or chest, causes a canine to achieve heights that are artificially high and can result in injury to less coordinated canines and puppies. If you have more than one canine, never play with them at the same time. Serious injury can occur when two or more canines attempt to catch the same disc at the same time.

canine disc competition organizers will not allow young dogs to be entered in competition until they have reached a certain age. We view the issue this way. Puppies are like kids. They are extremely energetic. Puppies roughhouse, run and jump and generally go berserk

Sven Van Driessche

Rollers are a great way to get your dog to focus on the disc.

World Champion Jeff Stanaway experienced just this type of injury with one of his canines years before he won the World Championship. One day, while he was in his backyard with his older dog *Cody*, and 12-week-old puppy *Cory*, Stanaway absent-mindedly tossed a fetch toy to *Cody*. Like a freight train, 50-pound *Cody* ran right over puppy *Cory* at full speed. Stanaway, even though he was a novice disc dogger at the time, knew better — but made the toss without thinking. Unfortunately, the collision fractured *Cory's* hind leg very badly. The orthopedic surgeon that repaired *Cory's* injured leg informed Stanaway that his pup would never be able to engage in disc sports as Stanaway's other canines had. This was a heartbreaking experience for Stanaway as well as a very valuable lesson that he passes along to novices anytime he teaches a class or performs with his dogs. The good news is that *Cory*, after many months of therapy and recuperation, healed normally and regained full use of his damaged leg. Not only that, *Cory* went on to win the 2003 Hyperflite Skyhoundz Open Division World Championship!

2003 World Champions Jeff Stanaway and "Cory."

FINDING A PLACE TO PLAY

If you are just getting started with your puppy or adult canine, you can hold training sessions inside your home if you have a large carpeted space that can be temporarily cleared of obstructions such as coffee tables, and valuable family heirlooms. You won't retain the support of your spouse if you smash a cherished family memento or damage the furniture. Spousal support is something that will come in handy as you go gallivanting across the globe in search of glory with your dog, while your better half stays home with all seven of the children, your mother, and your pet python *Huggy Bear*.

When you do move outside you should search for a level grassy area that is free of debris, holes and other obstacles. If you don't have a suitable backyard, you must venture out to find public spaces in which to play with your canine. Until you have unfailing control over your pet, choose a fenced athletic field in case your buddy should make a run for it.

In a few major cities in the United States and elsewhere in the world, our four-legged friends are *caninus non gratis* in parks and public green spaces. However, even in the most inhospitable environs, it is possible to find a nice grassy spot in which to practice if you're persistent. When you finally do find the ideal practice spot, be respectful of the property owner or administrator. Don't frequent the same spot more than a few times a week. Be sure to clean up after your pet and, for that matter, clean up any mess that you might be blamed for — even if you didn't make it. Many cities now have dog parks where it is possible to take your pet off leash and play without consequence. As a general rule, we don't recommend dog parks because of the possibility of entanglements with canines that belong to park patrons who have yet to master a semblance of control over their rampaging beasts. Dog parks can be dangerous places for our disc dogs. If you have no other alternative, then go early before the throng arrives.

Resist the temptation to take your canine to a park that is clearly not dog friendly. We would advise against tak-

PRO TIP

Laying the Foundation — *Teaching our four-legged friends to be disc dogs may not always be easy, but a proper foundation in the basics is crucial if you want to become one with your dog at the park or in competition. Disc dog skills can be likened to a three-legged stool — retrieving, catching, and everything else! Of the three, retrieving is often the most significant challenge, especially for those new to the sport.*

If I could offer just one bit of advice for aspiring disc doggers, it would be this: Teach your dog retrieval before you teach anything else. When I began training my 3-month-old Border Collie puppy, it took about two weeks before retrieval became routine for her. Whether you want your dog to place the disc in your hand, or at your feet, here is the method that worked for me.

When just starting out, practice only in a safe fenced-in area. Once you have your canine's attention, make a roller toss. Praise your dog if it shows any interest in the disc. When, eventually, your canine grabs the disc be sure to praise your dog heartily. With disc in mouth, your dog may become a bit possessive. If your dog does not immediately come to you when you call her, give the come command one or two more times in the most animated and excited way that you can. If your dog refuses to return the disc, then immediately end the play session. Try again an hour or two later. The key concept that you want to instill in your puppy is that failure to return the disc automatically ends playtime. Do not give in to your dog and chase her around as this will only encourage the unwanted keep-away behavior. When, at last, your dog brings the disc all the way to you, praise her vigorously and give her another roller toss as a reward. In a relatively short time, you will have a great retriever on your hands.

Training my puppy with a long line might also have worked — perhaps even faster. However, knowing the tendency of overly smart Border Collies to want to play keep away, it was important for me to instill in my young dog the idea that the more consistently she retrieved, the longer our play sessions would last. Since all canines appreciate playtime, this method is sure to work for almost anyone!

— Danny Eggleston, 2006 Hyperflite Skyhoundz Open Division World Champion

Peter Bloeme

Peter Bloeme

Shade of any kind, is always welcome to dogs on hot summer days.

ing your canine, for example, to Sheep Meadow in New York's Central Park where you are likely to have a very memorable encounter with New York's finest. If canines are not allowed to set paw in a particular park, then don't expect an exception to be made just because your canine happens to be a crowd-pleasing all-star. Find another venue. There are always nice areas closer than you think. If you find yourself in the all-too-familiar situation of being accosted by *the man*, be nice, apologize for your trans-

gression and enlist the help of the very fellow who has put the pinch on you and *Rover. But sir,* you can ask politely, *I can't find anyplace to play with my faithful friend and I have searched far and wide — have you any suggestions?* If the formality thing seems to work, then toss in this sure winner. *Kind Sir, I beseech thee to help a poor wretch, and her mangy mutt, find peace through vigorous exercise.* Anyway, you get the idea. Be polite, respectful and apologize profusely for your inadvertent lapse in judgment. You will probably survive with a friendly admonition. If you are warned, don't go back to the same park for a few months lest ye be smitten from above.

In the suburbs, many corporations will have large manicured green spaces that are ideal for disc play. In the eve-

A safe workout area is in everyone's best interest.

ning hours, only the occasional security guard will remain and they typically are busy watching sports on their *security monitors*. You may get run off from some of these spots too, but you likely won't be accosted by the gendarmerie. If you are approached, the absence of signs prohibiting your behavior…coupled with the improvised dumb look on your face…will usually save the day.

When all else fails, you can always try your local, elementary, middle, or high school. Most schools, public and private, have green space that you can borrow for 10 or 15 minutes occasionally, when the schools are closed. After all, you're a taxpayer for cryin' out loud, and your dogs are your children, right? Avoid the enticing green grass of the school football stadium. If the coach catches you on *his* grass, he may gouge you a new orifice or, worse yet, make you and Fido run wind sprints! You might try volunteering to do a half-time show or presentation for the kiddies to curry favor with school administrators. As long as you clean up after your dog and don't let your mongrel run wild, you will be amazed at how receptive most schools can be.

Having multiple practice locales for your canine will provide backup fields for emergencies and keep you from wearing out your welcome at any one site. No matter where you play or practice, it's always a good idea to schedule your practices at inconspicuous times. Just before sunset is a great time because most other

Please kind sir. Can we play here? We'll give you a donut...

park patrons have left for the day. It's also cooler and you can complete your practice session without having to stop and rest your dog.

ENVIRONMENTAL CONDITIONS

Pay attention to temperature and humidity when you are working out. Remember, even in the summer, your dog wears a fur coat. Whether your dog has short or long hair, it's easy for him to get overheated in warm weather because he cannot sweat (as humans do) to dissipate heat. Panting is the dog's primary method of internal cooling and it is not nearly as efficient as sweating. Never leave your dog locked in a car even with the windows open. On a warm day an automobile can quickly turn into an oven. Even a short stay inside a parked car can be dangerous. For example, the temperature inside your car on an 85 °F day can reach 100 °F in less than 10 minutes. In 30 minutes, the temperature will reach 120 °F — even with the windows slightly open. A dog can only stand temperatures like these for a very short time before suffering heat stroke, irreparable brain damage or death.

If you take your canine to the beach, then special precautions are in order. According to the Humane Society, dogs should not be taken to the beach between 10 am and 4 pm. That is when the sun's rays are the strongest and dogs are the most susceptible to heat stroke. If you plan to bring your dog with you to the beach, rent an umbrella to help keep him cool. The pads of a canine's paws have just as many nerves as human feet. So if the sand feels hot to you, it will feel hot to your dog.

Dogs love to romp in the surf with a disc, but saltwater is not for drinking. Be sure to bring fresh water from home for him. We once observed a canine happily lapping up salt water as it swam in the ocean. We warned the pet owner of the consequences but were informed that *Rebel drinks saltwater all the time.* A little while later, just after *Rebel* was loaded into the back seat of the family car, *Rebel* experienced a *rapid decompression.* That is to say, the poor creature simultaneously experienced

Peter Bloeme

Doesn't that look refreshing?

fire-hose vomiting and explosive diarrhea contained largely in the interior of the car. It was one of those rare *I-told-you-so* moments that we could have done without seeing.

Saltwater is also harsh on your canine's exterior in that it has a pronounced drying effect on canine skin. Bathe your dog with a mild shampoo when you get home from the beach. This will also help remove the embedded sand from his coat.

In the summertime when the weather is hot (know the tune?) consider reducing the duration of your play sessions. If you are fortunate enough to have a pond, lake, or slow-moving river near your practice field, you will be amazed at how quickly your dog can be cooled off by a dip in the water. It goes without saying that broken glass and debris tossed into such bodies of water can injure your pet, so consider the location of your swimming spot. Boat

Peter Bloeme (Sequence)

Water retrieving is a great low-impact method of conditioning for your disc dog.

ramps are bad swimming spots because jagged concrete, hidden underwater, can cause injury. Careless anglers drop all manner of things from their boats at ramp areas including glass bottles, beer cans, and fish hooks. Choose a spot that is unlikely to have once been a dumping spot for household appliances and other junk. If you live in the deep south, don't swim your dog at all. Alligators can snatch dogs that weigh 100 pounds or more without breaking a sweat. A lake or pond that was alligator free yesterday, may not be today. Crikey! It's just not worth the risk.

Ah, fortunately, hot weather doesn't last all year long. For some, cold weather is the issue. Depending on your dog's coat and general tolerance for exposure to cold weather, he will be more or less inclined to enjoy being outside in the winter. Keep in mind that too much play in the cold can cause frostbite while sidewalks that have been salted to melt ice and snow might burn sensitive dog paws, especially if they are raw from play sessions on abrasive-hard snow. Most flying discs will become more rigid when exposed to frigid temperatures.

Peter Bloeme

Don't make your dog go looking for water. Not having opposing thumbs makes this difficult.

Some will shatter like clay pigeons when your canine grabs them in flight.

LINK Hyperflite created the Frost-Bite disc for winter play http://hyperflite.com/frostbitediscs.html. It remains soft and flexible and won't shatter in temperatures well below 0 °F. If you have older-style discs that aren't cold-weather proof, try putting a hot water bottle in your disc bag and mak-

Sven Van Driessche

Disc dog events are a great way to socialize your dog with other dogs, fellow competitors, and spectators.

ing only a few throws before you place the disc in the bag to be re-warmed.

SOCIALIZATION

In the course of your canine disc training, make an effort to ensure that your pet will get along with strangers and the other dogs that he will inevitably encounter in parks or at disc dog competitions. Begin socializing your dog as a puppy by getting him around lots of people (adults and children) and dogs at fairs, parks, and puppy training classes. Any signs of aggressive behavior should be taken seriously and properly dealt with. There are many excellent training guides that deal with the various forms of canine aggression and other behavioral disorders. Don't wait until a correctable problem turns into an ingrained behavior.

Jeff Perry

Peter Bloeme believes strongly in socialization as he introduces a little "Magic" to the Dallas Cowboy cheerleaders.

An example of a homemade long line.

Peter Bloeme

TRAINING WITH A LONG LINE

It is often helpful to train your disc dog with an ultra-long leash sometimes referred to as a long line. This is an item that is easily made with a laundry cord, flat ½ inch webbing, or 5-8 mm climbing cord that can be purchased from an outdoor store. A long line should be 15-30 feet in length. Using a figure eight knot or a bowline knot, you can add a loop for your hand on one end of the long line if you wish. On the other end of the long line, securely attach a dog clip (just like those found on most leashes) that you can find at your local hardware store. Be especially careful of two things when using a long line. First, make sure that your dog doesn't become tangled in the line during training. Never use a long line until it is free of knots and tangles or you might injure your pet. Second, be aware of the possibility of rope burn. If your canine runs past you and the long line drags against your exposed skin, expect a nasty surprise. Webbing seems to be a little less likely than cord to cause burns so choose it first if available.

A long line is commonly used to develop long-range verbal control. Controlling your dog like a professional not only ensures good performances, it may also prevent unfortunate confrontations with people, cars, and other dogs. If your young canine should make a break for it, it is much easier to catch part of the trailing long line than the canine.

Occasionally, even experienced disc doggers have to retrain disc dogs that develop controlling tendencies like keep-

MicroDogs and puppies do best when you work at their level.

Sven Van Driessche

Step One: Help your dog to become comfortable with the disc by feeding and watering him from it.

Step Two: Tease your canine with gentle tug-of-war-play.

away behavior. A long line is perfect for reinforcing proper retrieval behavior.

TRACKING

Tracking is simply the practical ability to follow a moving object. With dogs, tracking is instinctive and natural, but it does take time for the instinct to mature and some dogs become better at it than others.

An example of tracking in human development is a child's ability to catch. At first it looks like the child is closing his or her hands randomly and will never catch anything. With practice, a child's tracking ability improves and the child can start to predict the path of a moving object and make successful catches.

A young puppy is very much like a small child in that it may seem completely unable to track the path of a moving object. If you toss something over a puppy's head, then as far as the puppy is concerned, that object no longer exists. It's as if it disappeared by magic. Ultimately, nearly all puppies and canines are capable of developing excellent tracking skills. With puppies, you

can speed the acquisition of tracking behavior by rolling a ball, disc or favorite chew toy back and forth in front of him. You might also make gentle, low-level tosses a small distance from your puppy so that he can follow the toy or treat easily. Praise and reward your puppy for exhibiting tracking behavior and, very quickly, the puppy will be locking onto its targets like a heat-seeking missile.

CATCHING

The all important catch phase of training is often the most rewarding. It's sort of like a child's first steps. Things will happen quickly for you and your canine after that first catch.

If you've had success in getting your dog to chase and grab rollers and sliders then it's time to master the catch. To optimize your chances for success you must first elevate your canine's excitement level. Become over-animated and ebullient in the way you relate to your pet as you teach the all-important *catch* of the disc. Using the same disc that you used for rollers and sliders, start by teasing your canine with gentle tug-of-

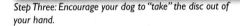

Step Three: Encourage your dog to "take" the disc out of your hand.

Step Four: Make short roller tosses to your dog.

war play, keep-away, rollers, and upside-down sliders. Really *fire-him-up* so that he will want the disc. Once you have his attention and you've established an elevated excitement level, kneel down in front of your dog and continue rapidly moving the disc near your canine's face to keep him focused on the prize. Be careful not to whack him with the disc in your excitement! Next, let your canine try and grab the disc from your hand. Let go at the last second. Reward a successful grab by letting him hold the disc in his mouth for a few seconds. If he doesn't actually grab the disc, and it falls to the ground, praise him for the effort but do not let him have the disc. He gets to keep it, only if he catches it. Once your canine is consistently grabbing the disc from your hand, try gently tossing the disc near your canine. **Never** toss the disc directly at your canine. Instead, toss the disc as a pizza chef might toss a pizza — level and straight up in the air. Put lots of spin on it and make it hover tantalizingly close to your canine. You should start your *pizza tosses*

from ground level and they should rise no higher than your canine's eye level. When *Rover* finally catches a toss, be liberal with the praise, let him hold his prize for a few seconds as a reward, and then gently take the disc from him and toss it again.

Success is a wonderful thing.

Peter Bloeme (Sequence)

After your dog is chasing rollers consistently you can progress to short tosses.

You may have some difficulty getting your canine to give the disc back now that he has finally caught it. This is the perfect time to work on your release command. Most disc doggers use the universal *drop* command. The *drop* command is discussed in greater detail in the following chapter, but here are the basics. To begin with, try giving the *drop* command repeatedly until your dog lets go of the disc on its own. When he does, praise him and say *good drop* and immediately make another toss to him. He will soon learn that, in order to get another throw, he must release the disc he has in his mouth. You can accelerate his learning of the *drop* command by introducing multiple (up to five) discs into the mix. Often, when a canine sees a second disc in your hand, he will drop the one he is holding so that you will throw the next disc to him. In between tosses, give the *drop* command until he lets go of the disc. If he drops the previous disc as you have commanded, reward him with another toss. Using more than one disc will get your canine comfortable with the concept of *multiples* which you will find useful if you decide to compete. In Skyhoundz Freestyle competitions, up to five discs may be used at a time.

From *pizza tosses* you can advance to longer and longer throws. Initially, try and make your throws into the wind so that your canine will have time to catch

Sven Van Driessche

Multiples help to reinforce the "catch" and "drop" commands.

Amy King demonstrates a short pizza toss to her dog.

Peter Bloeme

up to the disc, throttle down, and make a nice leaping catch. Don't attempt long throws until you have mastery of short and mid-range tosses.

WARM-UPS

Dogs are like humans in that they perform better when they have an opportunity to warm up before engaging in vigorous athletic activity. Some disc doggers even go so far as to manually stretch their canines before play. On cold days or anytime your pet has been idle for an extended period, it is always wise to warm him up before going all out. Start with a short leash walk followed by a few gentle low-level disc tosses. If all goes well, then make a few slightly higher tosses designed to encourage jumps. On hot days, a short warm-up, is about all your canine will need. In colder weather, you may want to make a few long throws to make sure your dog is adequately warmed

up. Use common sense and don't even think about playing or competing if you detect signs of injury or soreness during your warm up.

JUMPING

Many veterinarians recommend that you don't encourage your canine to jump until he is between 12 and 18 months-of-age. However, we all know that most canines will jump whether we like it or not. In fact, if you try and keep an energetic young canine from running, jumping and carousing, it will probably explode. Short of chaining your canine to the ground, there is no real way to prevent jumping behavior. In our experience, jumping behavior, in and of itself, rarely causes injuries. After all, it's not the jumping that causes the injuries, it's the landing! We suggest the application of logic and reason to the problem. First, evaluate your disc dog candidate, whether young or old. How athletic and coordinated is your canine? How focused and obedient? Is the dog trim or a little overweight? The answers to these questions will guide you in determining whether your beginning disc dog or puppy is ready to learn tricks that involve jumping.

Vaulting is another matter. Just to be clear — under no circumstances should you vault a canine until: 1) it is at least 18 months of age, 2) the canine has been checked for genetic predisposition to hip displasia (a chronic problem for German Shepherds and certain other breeds), 3) the canine has developed adequate coordination and good spatial awareness, and 4) you have received hands-on instruction from an expert trainer who comes well recommended by other experienced disc doggers. Vaults, are not necessary for success in competition and they increase the possibility of serious injury. You don't have

This is what I call a dog's life...I can't wait for the mud packs...

Sven Van Driessche

to do them to win a canine disc World Championship title. If you do choose to perform vaults, have your dog jump far, rather than high. Either type of vault is spectacular if well executed and the

Once your dog is consistently catching short throws you can begin to try longer tosses.

Jeff Hoot

It's natural for dogs to love to jump.

long *vaults* are generally safer than the high ones.

So, what do you do if your canine doesn't want to jump? Simple. First, recognize that there may be many reasons that your canine might not jump naturally. For example, if your canine is packing a few extra pounds, it may not feel like jumping. Certain breeds, like Blue Tick Coon Hounds jump naturally as if they've cornered a raccoon in a tree. You wouldn't expect Saint Bernards to be good jumpers by virtue of their size and less-than-speedy approach to just about everything. Most dogs are fully capable of jumping if you give them a reason to do it. A treat might be just such a reason. If you have a dog that is not yet hooked on the disc and you want to encourage jumping, try running with a treat held in your hand at a challenging height for your canine. Why run, you might ask? Jumping while running is safer than vertical jumping because canines are less likely to injure themselves in a striding jump. If you encourage your canine to jump,

and he does so, then praise and reward him (either with the disc or a treat) for the effort. Remember, initially, it is not important that your canine catch the disc or grab the treat — it's only important

Gotcha!

A great example of a safe low "vault."

that he makes the effort when you give the command. You can also encourage jumping by holding a disc above your outstretched arm or leg. If you have to, lay on the floor, hold a disc in the air above and beyond your outstretched leg, and encourage your canine to step over you. Hold the disc higher each time and eventually, he will get the hang of it. Some canines will try and go around you to get the disc. If need be, enlist the support of a helper who can lead the dog over you as you give the *jump* command.

You might also try encouraging your canine to jump through a Hula Hoop. The Hula Hoop is great because it is non-threatening, lightweight, and plenty big enough for your dog to jump through. Start low and work your way up to higher and higher jumps. Use a disc or treat for bait until your canine gets the idea. Be sure to give the *jump* command consistently when you want your dog to become airborne.

Finally, there is no better way to teach a dog to jump than to make good short throws into the wind with lots of spin. Throwing into the wind will cause a disc to hover in the air in front of your dog. Eventually, old *Spike* will grow tired of waiting for the disc to drop down to his level. Instead, he'll reach up and grab it. When that happens, sing out with praise and make a huge deal about it. Try and repeat the behavior as soon as possible by making the same kind of throw that induced the first jump. Before you know it, jumping will be as natural to your canine as feathers on a duck.

COMMON CANINE INJURIES

When you use common sense, canine disc play is exceedingly safe. Injuries of any kind are rare. When they do occur it is usually because of a mistake that we make. Bad throws cause canines to run into things. Our failure to properly police the playing field can cause a ca-

Come to papa!

Thorn Gillott

Sven Van Driessche

Everyone loves a great jumper!

nine to step in a hole or cut a paw on a foreign object. Overworking a canine on a hot day can contribute to heat stroke or heat exhaustion.

One common, but extremely minor disc-related injury is the dreaded *tongue bite*. When dog's are hot, they extend their canine radiators (tongues) to cool off. When your panting canine starts to chomp down on a disc without fully *reeling in* his tongue, bleeding is the inevitable result. These minor tongue nicks can look awful because, like shaving cuts, they bleed like the dickens. Mix a little blood with dog slobber, add a flapping tongue, and in an instant, your disc dog can look like a character in an Alfred Hitchcock movie. Once, Hyperflite was contacted by a disc dog newbie who thought her disc dog was suffering from internal bleeding that had begun to pour out of the canine's mouth. The cure for the tongue bite is simple and

nearly instantaneous. Merely allow your canine to drink a little cold water (ice water is best) and the bleeding will stop very quickly. After the bleeding stops it's sometimes hard to find the injury that caused all the red stuff in the first place. If the bleeding doesn't stop quickly, or if it appears to be coming from somewhere other than the canine's tongue, check with your vet to be on the safe side. A bleeder is almost never a big deal — unless you're performing in front of a group of school kids! Once your dog cools down, you can start practicing or playing again. If your dog seems to have the bleeding problem a little too frequently, then you are most likely engaging in overly-long play sessions during the hottest part of the day. Extended tongues are easy to bite and injure by accident. Try and schedule your practice sessions during the cooler parts of summer days. Take frequent breaks and give your canine lots of cool water. Rest between practice sessions — until your dog is no longer panting.

Another common injury generator is the tendency of disc dog enthusiasts to push their canines too quickly when they are recovering from muscle pulls and other minor injuries. Sometimes, it is the canine that pushes the owner to get back to disc dog play after a long lay-off. The one who wears the skirt or the pants must take charge and keep a minor injury from turning into a major one. Follow your vet's advice and don't work your recuperating dog until it has had time to heal. Then, gradually work back up to your normal activities.

Our involvement in canine disc sports spans many decades and one of the saddest things that we hear about is canines that are struck by cars. Please, don't practice near highways or roads. Equally important is the concept of leashing your canine at all times when you aren't on the playing field. That includes the 30 feet between your car and your front door. There is a tendency, once you have a well-trained canine, to allow off-leash walking in places where 99.9% of the time, your dog will follow your commands. Unfortunately, cats and squirrels and other enticements can show up when you don't expect them and lure your precious family member into the street just as a car speeds by. It's an awful thing to witness and we implore you to take every precaution with your canine to prevent this type of tragedy.

Now, we've told you about all the obvious things that can happen to your canine, but there is one more, not-so-obvious, affliction that may take years before it begins to produce observable symptoms. That affliction is skin cancer. Disc dogs spend a lot of time in the sun and, sadly, the Earth's protective ozone layer is not what it once was. There are several companies that make sunscreen products that can protect vulnerable areas on your pet from exposure to the harsh rays of the sun. Lest you think that your pop-up canopy cover will protect your dog, think again. Even indirect, reflected, exposure to ultraviolet radiation can be harmful to your canine.

Forewarned is forearmed, the expression goes, and now that you know what to expect, we trust that your canine will enjoy many years of disc dog fun — without injury.

COMMON HUMAN INJURIES

Avoiding injury is something we usually think of in the context of our canines but, increasingly, we have seen trainers

"Takes" are often used in training to teach canines to jump on or over a trainer's body.

Peter Bloeme

suffer from an assortment of injuries. Thus, we thought it prudent to devote a few paragraphs to the human side of the equation. To begin with, canine disc play is an athletic endeavor. You should, therefore, take reasonable precautions and utilize appropriate equipment if you are going to participate in this activity. First, wear athletic shoes. Bare feet, sandals, flip flops, and other inappropriate shoes are an invitation to pain. It may seem like a 60's kind of thing to do — toss a flying disc to your dog with soft green grass between your toes — but you will think differently the first time a canine pushes off of, or runs across, your foot as it digs in to chase down a disc. The pain is a cross between a hornet sting and what we imagine hot molten lead would feel like if it were poured onto the top of your foot.

Dentists love disc doggers because we do smart things like hold flying discs in our mouths while canines race toward us at 35 miles per hour. We almost always let go of the disc before the canine arrives — almost always. If you must perform tricks like the *jawbreaker*, as it is aptly known, practice it first by holding the disc in your hand near your mouth just to make sure you have the timing down pat.

Lower back injuries are also becoming increasingly common among top disc dog competitors who often catch their canines while they are airborne. If you catch your canine in the course of performing one of these tricks be

Cynthia Tobin

We discourage playing with more than one dog at a time, but this is just too cute!

sure not to lean forward. As you catch *Phydeaux*, bend your knees slightly so that your legs, rather than your spine will absorb the impact.

Leading the parade of canine disc related injuries that occur to bi-peds (that's us humans) are those that result from the performance of vaulting tricks. *Vaults*, although spectacular to spectators, are not required for success in competition. But folks keep on doing them anyway. And people keep getting hurt. In the interest of good taste we won't recount these injuries in specific detail except to say that one such injury that happened to a male disc dogger caused a feature of the male anatomy that is normally the size of a walnut to swell to grapefruit size. Female disc doggers

have suffered injury to the unprotected upper-frontal realms of the female anatomy with even greater frequency. *Vaults* are covered in greater detail in the chapter that follows. Generally speaking, you should never attempt a *vault* until you have a chance to work with an expert trainer who can help keep you and your canine from getting injured. When dogs push off of your body their claws can make you look as if you were given 20 lashes, even if you were wearing a thick shirt. If you decide to perform *vaulting* tricks, wear appropriate protective gear including, vaulting vests, thigh protectors and the special protective gear made just for us fellows.

Always make sure you keep your head out of the way of your dog's body and claws.

LINK Specialized neoprene vaulting vests (similar to scuba diving vests) are available through the Skyhoundz store http://skyhoundz.com/store.html.

As disc doggers become more creative in the tricks that they create and in their attempts to distinguish themselves from their fellow competitors on the playing field, injuries are inevitable. If we respect the premise that canine disc play is an athletic endeavor for human as well as canine, and we take appropriate action to lessen the possibility of injury, we can expect to enjoy many years of fun with our canine companions.

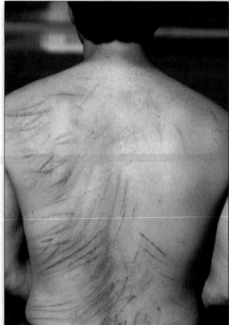

Not some medieval torture session or the result of dropping chewing gum on the ground in Singapore. This is an example of why wearing a neoprene vaulting vest would be preferable to a T-shirt when doing "back vaults."

Lawrence Frederick receives a "paw tatoo" on his cheek. "Danger Will Robinson!"

Jeff Hoo

A fast retrieve is critical to a high Distance/Accuracy score.

Disc Dogs! Advanced

Once the basics are mastered, you will undoubtedly want to attempt more difficult tricks with your dog. By the time Disc Dogs! is published, there will already be new tricks and moves being created by elite-level disc doggers and by folks that want to become elite-level disc doggers. Innovation, we have always maintained, is what separates the great teams from the merely good teams. No matter what your personal goals may be, it is fun to create a new move or trick that nobody else can do…yet!

LINK Since the trick sequences involved in advanced training can sometimes be complex, you might find our companion DVD, *Disc Dog: Training DVD*, or one of the many DVD offerings available through the Skyhoundz store http://skyhoundz.com/store.html, to be useful. If you are the least bit hazy as to how to perform a particular trick, one of these DVD offerings should help make it all perfectly clear.

A nice reverse overhand wrist-flip toss to a small dog.

Sven Van Driessche

When describing advanced maneuvers we may, for convenience, relate to you a stance or start position commonly used for the trick. You are not limited to the start position that we describe. For example, *vaults* are typically initiated with the trainer in a standing position. However, they can just as easily (and perhaps more safely) be performed with the trainer in a kneeling or squatting position. Similarly, *back-* *flips* are typically performed with a trainer kneeling to accentuate the height of the canine. However, you may also stand to deliver *backflip* throws or even lie on your back and deliver the discs with a foot toss. Once again, you will be limited only by your imagination. We encourage you to experiment. You may just surprise yourself and develop the coolest trick in the world!

A demonstration of a low "back vault."

Jeff Perry

A basic "take" is simply a trick in which your dog takes the disc out of your hand.

TAKE

Although you will not directly receive credit in competition for a *take*, the concept is invaluable as a versatile training technique. To learn the *take* start your practice session by getting your dog excited about playing. Then hold the disc in the air, slightly above him, and say *take*. When he goes for it let him take the disc out of your hand and hang onto it for a moment. Praise your canine for a successful *take* and then give the *drop* command. You can gradually raise the disc higher and higher until it's well over his head. This is also a useful way of warming him up and strengthening his legs.

Later on, this command can be used when you want your dog to *take* the disc out of your mouth, from behind your head, or even from your hand as your canine leaps over your outstretched leg or arm. Once you have the *take* command mastered, you can begin to release the disc an instant be-

fore your canine takes it from your hand or mouth. Putting a little spin on the disc as you let it go will keep the disc stable until *Rover* grabs it. An early release ensures that judges will regard your tricks as throws rather than mere handoffs, which are typically not scored.

Sven Van Driessche

If you have a dog who is "height challenged," you should get down to his level.

A Pairs Freestyle version of the mouth "take."

Sven Van Driessche (Sequence)

Another variation you might want to try is having your dog take the disc out of your mouth. This potentially hazardous trick is referred to as the *Jawbreaker*. It is not generally dangerous for canines since they have harder heads than humans do! Make sure, before you attempt a *jawbreaker*, that your canine is able to consistently perform *takes* at close quarters without colliding with any part of your body...and that your dental insurance premiums are up-to-date. To teach the *jawbreaker*, position your canine a few paces away and facing in your direction. Next, turn sideways to your canine and hold a disc upside down in your hand about two feet in front of you, level with your mouth. If you hold the disc too close, initially, your canine may refuse to take the disc for fear that a collision with his best friend might ensue. Angle the disc toward your dog and give the *take* command. If you have

a smaller dog or puppy, you may have to start by kneeling or by widening your stance to get the disc at the right altitude for your canine. For the actual mouth *take*, rest a clean, dry disc upside down in your mouth. You'll find that it is much easier to hold a disc in your mouth if it is upside down. Although your canine will be approaching you from the side, watch him from the corner of your eye and, as he leaps, let go of the disc. If you forget to let go of the disc, it's fat-lip city at the good end of the spectrum and expensive dental work, a broken jaw, or worse at the bad end. Again, do not try and anticipate your canine's arrival, when he jumps, let the disc go. One interesting variation on the *jawbreaker* was performed by a World Champion in the late 80's. Instead of the familiar standing *jawbreaker*, this trainer would run sideways toward his canine while the canine ran toward him.

Glen Provenzano (Sequence)

"Mouth take" sequence by Mike Miller and "Pro."

At the last moment, the speeding canine would grab the disc just as it was released from the trainer's mouth. The timing on such a trick is critical and there is little room for miscalculation.

Another interesting variation on the *jawbreaker* was demonstrated by former world finalist Don Kent and his dog *Bandit*. The duo accomplished the standard *jawbreaker* with a twist. While *Bandit* sat patiently in the ready position,

Kent placed a disc in his mouth, then made a hoop with his arms. *Bandit* had to jump through the hoop while grabbing the *jawbreaker*. For larger canines the hoop can be enlarged nearly 18" by holding a disc in each hand.

Here are a few other tricks you can try that make use of the *take* command:

● Put the disc on your head (or on your dogs head) and have your canine take it.

Jeff Hoot (Sequence)

A "take" doesn't have to involve your hands. You can easily hold the disc with your feet.

The "take" technique can be used to teach your dog "overs." First photo is a back "over," while the second is an example of a front leg "over."

- Use the *take* command to bait your dog into jumping into your arms.
- From a kneeling or standing position, extend an arm laterally from your side; then have your dog take the disc from your other hand while jumping over your extended arm.
- From the standing position extend one leg and have your canine take the disc as he jumps over your extended leg. Then, make a little hop and switch legs (a.k.a. scissors kick) as your canine returns in the opposite direction. Remember to toss the disc in the air with a little *pizza toss* so that the judges will score the trick.

World Champion Jeff Perry ends his routine with an advanced "take" by having "Gilbert" jump into his arms. Notice that Perry releases the disc before "Gilbert" catches it.

To encourage your dog to jump, you can hold the disc out and use the "take" command.

For mouth "takes" let go before your dog grabs the disc.

Another example of a hand "take."

THE DROP COMMAND

Now that we've covered the *take* command, it's time to mention its equally-important counterpart — *drop*. Some dogs will naturally drop the disc at your feet while others need to have discs virtually pried out of their mouths with a *Jaws of Life*. Since most folks don't have access to a pneumatic spreader, it's easier if your dog learns, from the get-go, to release the disc on command.

To teach the *drop* command, have your canine sit a few feet away as you kneel in front of him. Practice with a leash or long line if necessary to prevent your dog from running off. Once you have your dog's attention, make a short toss and let him grab the disc. Then, with as much authority as you can muster, say *drop*. If he doesn't readily let go, gently pinch the sides of his mouth against his teeth with your free hand while grasping the disc firmly in your other hand. This is an uncomfortable position for your dog so he will likely open his mouth and release the disc. Praise him when he does and repeat the sequence until he drops the disc on command without the physical inducement. Once you have the *drop* command down, try making a short toss to your dog. After he catches the disc, prepare to make a toss with a second disc and then give the *drop* command. Do not throw the sec-

If one person isn't enough to get your dog to release the disc, you might want to try a second. Actually, in this case, "Wallace" has been taught "not" to let go. Good thing he is using a "Jawz disc!"

Sven Van Driessche

ond disc until your canine drops the disc he's holding in his mouth. Continue to repeat the *drop* command a few times if necessary. When your canine drops the disc, reward him with another toss. With practice, you should be able to use the *drop* command to cause your canine to immediately let go of a disc anywhere on the field. Before long, your canine will be on *auto drop* as he realizes that the only way to get another toss from you is to release the disc that he is holding. Multiples, discussed later in this chapter, are also a great way to reinforce the *drop* command.

"Drop" is a very important command to teach your dog.

A double "Merry-Go-Round" in Pairs Freestyle.

OVER

Over is a versatile command that can be used in two ways. It can simply be a stand-alone trick or it can be used as a stepping stone to, or component of, more advanced tricks. Once your dog knows this command, you can have him jump over your leg, back, head, etc., depending on his leaping ability. A word of caution for doing *overs* with your leg extended — always extend the leg that is closest to your dog. This affords your vital areas some protection in the event that your canine collides with you or tries to push off of your body while going for the disc.

To perform a basic leg *over*, position your canine a few yards away. Then kneel or sit on the ground with one leg extended. Hold the disc over your leg and give the command *over*. Always hold the disc in the opposite hand for better balance. For example, for a standing leg *over* made with the left leg extended, hold the disc in your right

hand. If necessary give the disc a waggle to pique your dog's interest. Your canine should move to the disc and jump over your outstretched leg. If your canine is a good jumper and easily clears your leg, you can try standing and extending the leg closest to your canine. Hold the disc above your leg and give the *over* command. If it looks as if your canine is not going to clear your leg, you can lower it at the last second.

The occasional canine will refuse to jump over your body for fear of accidentally injuring you. Canines are smart that way! If your canine refuses to jump over your body or circles around you, you may have to have a helper guide him over the first few times on leash. If necessary, practice close to a wall or fence, to keep your canine from going around, instead of over, your outstretched limb. As with training any new trick, breaking things down into small steps will help your canine get the big picture a bit faster. A few *overs* with a friend leading your canine over your out-

Here you have a prone "over."

Larry Beatty demonstrates a kneeling leg "over."

Sven Van Driessche

Sven Van Driessche

After you get your dog to commit to an "over," you can pull your leg back out of the way if necessary.

Jeff Hoot (Sequence)

stretched leg, for example, coupled with hearty praise and some roughhousing, will likely convince your canine that it is OK to jump in close proximity to your body. Once you have mastered the *over* in one direction, have your canine return in the opposite direction. After all, you want your canine to be *ambijumpsterous* (it's a real word, just look in any disctionary).

Overs are the bread and butter of many disc dog routines. They can help you demonstrate your canine's leaping ability, quickness, and agility, all in close proximity to your body. They can, if creatively performed, be real crowd pleasers. We never cease to be amazed at the endless variety of *overs* that are demonstrated by competing teams

A full body "over."

Sven Van Driessche

A leg "over."

Sven Van Driessche

each year. Further, close interaction with your canine will help boost your score in Presentation or Wow!Factor categories in Freestyle. Since props are not allowed in canine disc competitions, in essence, your body is the only prop that you have. Adding a *Cirque de Soleil* aspect to your trick sequences employing the venerable *over*, is well within the grasp of novice disc doggers if you are persistent in your training and creative in your choreography.

Tracy Custer demonstrates a variation of the "over" by laying down on the ground and flipping the disc over her body as "Raccoon Jack" jumps to make the catch.

Overs can be combined with two-handed throws, butterfly throws, multiple disc throws, and with unusual deliveries including knife-edge tosses, kick throws, and even mouth throws. You can even *interrupt* an *over* by catching your dog just as it catches the disc. In fact, just when we begin to think that we've seen them all, a novice competitor will come along and remind us that it's never too late to show us *old dogs* a new trick.

Peter Bloeme and "Wizard" demonstrate a reverse leg "over."

It's nice to meet you...what a lovely dog you have!

MULTIPLES

Simply put, multiples are a series of rapid throws of any type made to a canine. Current competition rules for the Hyperflite Skyhoundz World Canine Disc Championship Series allow up to five discs to be used in a Freestyle routine. Multiples can be a series of several short throws or a grouping of long floating tosses that allow a canine time to zigzag across the playing field, catching one after another.

Teaching your dog to catch multiples requires that your canine have a good understanding of the *drop* command. A canine should be able to catch and immediately drop discs in succession in anticipation of the next throw. Once a canine gets the hang of a particular multiple sequence, he will usually hold onto

One throw immediately after another spells multiples.

your last toss while you gather up the remaining discs to prepare for the next grouping of tricks and/or throws. Initially, it may be helpful to alert your canine, with a consistent command, that another throw is on the way. Some trainers use alert commands like *another, come'n at you,* or *watch* to keep their canines focused and anticipating another toss. Three-time World Championship team Bill Murphy and *Bouncin' Boo,* performed a long-range multiple sequence that featured three discs in the air, simultaneously. While his dog ran from one side of the field to the other catching each disc, Murphy yelled, with a Texas drawl, *Nuther One — Nuther One — Nuther One.* Long-range blind multiples are spectacular and energizing to crowds when they work. But, if your timing is off, your canine may end up running from one miss to another.

Alert commands almost always serve double duty as *drop* commands.

You can use two hands for multiples and alternate throws from one hand to the other.

Terri Hanson

Peter Bloeme and "Wizard" demonstrate vertical multiples. The discs move so quickly that one is usually in the air while "Wizard" is catching another.

GRAVY

I was working with an Australian Shepherd rescue group and had recently become involved in canine disc sports. I found an ad in the paper regarding an Australian Shepherd that an older couple just couldn't handle so I went to visit him. It turned out that the "Aussie" was actually a Cattle Dog mix! When I first saw him he was in the backyard chewing on a disc. The elderly couple said that "he just liked to chew on them."

They also shared with me the Cattle Dog's history. Apparently, he was adopted first by a vet tech as a puppy and then adopted out to a family when she couldn't handle him. The family couldn't handle him either, given his propensity for chasing kids on bikes, etc. And so, the little Cattle Dog mix was already with his third adoptive family but hadn't yet found a home.

I told them I would help them out even though he wasn't the Australian Shepherd I had been expecting. I took him home and have never looked back. We had "Captain Jack" catching a disc out of the air within 24 hours. It took a little bit longer to get him to let go! Our Captain Jack became a champion disc catcher and competes with both my son and me. We love him more than words can say!

— *Christina Curtis, aka "Captain Jack's" mom*

Jeff Perry (Sequence)

Hyperflite Skyhoundz World Finalist Theresa Musi gets "Ciela Azule" to balance on one of Musi's feet, in a "stall," while she

By that we mean, that a command like *another* should cause your dog to prepare to drop the disc he is holding because another one is coming fast! Alert commands can also be very useful when your canine isn't looking at you when you throw. Since discs make very little noise when in flight, there are only two ways that a dog will know that you have made another throw. He must either see the disc as you release it, or acquire it visually after you give him an alert command. Some trainers go so far as to give their dogs directional alert commands like *left, right,* or *high*. These specific alert commands can help your dog determine where to look for a disc, especially if the canine is running away from you when you make your throw. Say, for example, that you are attending a Hyperflite Xtreme Distance Challenge event with your dog *Blaze*. You've just sent *Blaze* off for a really long one. But, oops, you hook the throw to the left. A timely *left* command will alert your

2007 Hyperflite Skyhoundz Open Division World Champion Danny

canine that he should look over his left shoulder for the disc. To train left, right, high, etc., just make throws that fit that description and give the corresponding command to your canine. He will get the hang of it quickly.

delivers a series of upside-down multiples.

Venegas, delivers a series of multiples to his standing canine.

Jeff Perry (Sequence)

Eventually, as you practice specific freestyle sequences with your canine, he will begin to anticipate your actions and alert commands will become unnecessary. However, when training new sequences, he may need some prompting with those commands to get the hang of things. It's always a good idea to practice alert commands occasionally for reinforcement.

More Multiples...

Sven Van Driessche (Sequence)

Multiple tosses can be made straight to your dog.

Sven Van Driessche (Sequence)

Multiple tosses can also be made while your canine circles you.

MULTIPLE
DISC CATCHES

Not to be confused with multiples are multiple disc catches. On short distance moves such as *takes*, *overs*, and *backflips*, it is possible to release two or more discs at the same time so that your canine can catch them simultaneously. Bulldog breeds and other hard biting, large-mouthed, canines are very good at snagging more than one disc at a time. Although you don't see much of it in competition these days, World Champion canines, in years gone by, could routinely catch two or more discs, thrown simultaneously, with a variety of deliveries.

Some dogs will even catch one disc after another without dropping them. The best known multiple disc catching canine was *Zeuss,* trained by Craig Brownell, who could hold nine discs in his mouth at once. He is listed in the *Guinness Book of World Records*! As cool looking as this trick is, you risk

Nice two-disc grab!

turning your canine into a *one-trick pony* if you encourage him to catch additional discs without dropping the previous catch first.

Craig Brownell's dog "Zeuss" demonstrates that eight is definitely enough!

A red bow tie nicely complements a black tux and "tail."

FLIPS

The *flip* is arguably the most spectacular example of canine athleticism. A well-executed twisting *flip*, coupled with a seemingly impossible catch and a great landing, is nothing less than awe inspiring. *Flips* are common in competition and, fortunately, they are fairly simple to teach. *Flips* can be performed in either direction. In years gone by, *flips* to the right were called *backflips* and *flips* to the left were called *frontflips*. However, distinguishing between the two is only necessary if you want to cue your canine that he is expected to jump in one direction or another.

"Backflip:" Peter Bloeme uses the roller delivery to make a

Some canines will *flip* naturally if a disc is thrown in just the right fashion. However, to ensure consistency, disc doggers should teach the *flip* as they do any other trick. Despite its advanced appearance, teaching the *flip* is actually pretty simple. Start by kneeling with your dog facing you. Ideally, your canine should be in a sitting position about three feet away from you.

As you prepare to make a throw to your canine, say the word *flip* so that your canine will associate the command with the type of throw you will be making to him. Next, make a knife-edge throw above and slightly to one side of your dog. Generally speaking, a right-handed throw should be made to the right of your canine. The object, initially, is to get your dog to lift his front feet off of the ground and follow the disc through an arcing trajectory. If you have thrown the disc high enough over your canine's head, he may actually lift his hind legs off the ground as he tries to grab the disc. If your canine merely watches as the disc sails over

"Frontflip:" Using a short vertical throw, Peter Bloeme

his head, then make lower throws to pattern the desired behavior. Gradually increase the height of your tosses as your dog catches on. Once your canine is consistently picking his front feet off the ground, you can challenge him with higher and higher throws.

throw over "Wizard's" head. "Wizard" starts to leave the ground, spins, does the "flip" and makes the catch.

Walt Mancini (Sequence)

makes a toss over "Wizard's" head. "Wizard" jumps after the "bad" throw, spins, makes the catch, and lands safely.

Walt Mancini (Sequence)

Before you know it, you will have a flipping machine on your hands. This trick can almost always be taught in only a few training sessions. Most novice dogs that we have occasion to train during our clinics learn the *flip* in a few moments. If you are having trouble visualizing the technique for teaching the flip, find a copy of Hyperflite's *Disc Dog Training DVD* and you will be an expert in no time.

ust as in gymnastics, it's important to "spot" your dog when you are teaching a new trick like a "flip."

Unbelievable! "Crash" summersaults 360° and lands on his feet.

STALLS

Stalls, are a relatively recent phenomenon in disc dog competition. A *stall* is any human/canine interaction that causes a dog to jump onto, and pause on, some part of the anatomy of the human teammate. For example, a trainer on his hands and knees might command a dog to jump onto the trainer's back and pause for effect. Trick sequences must begin or end with a disc in flight in order to be scored, so, trainers that perform *stalls* usually make some sort of throw to their canines as they transition their dogs out of the *stall* and back to terra firma. Use a unique command so that your canine will know that it is time to perform the *stall*. The command might be as simple as *get on*. A helper can assist in positioning a canine on a trainer's body until the dog gets the hang of things.

Some top teams are now performing *stalls* in which a canine will stand on the soles of the trainer's shoes. To perform this type of foot *stall*, the trainer, obviously, must lie on her back with feet extended straight up to create a level platform. Rumor has it that a certain competitor taught this trick to her canine by wearing a pair of size 14 sneakers over her regular shoes. As soon as her dog got the hang of things, she merely switched back to her dainty tennies. Once in the stall position, throws are made straight up to a canine who may, for extra style points, dismount with a nice *backflip*. A well-executed *stall* of this nature is more impressive to spectators and judges than the nasty-old *vaults* discussed later in this chapter. *Stalls* are a great example of the ingenuity and innovation of modern disc doggers. It's only a matter of time before someone tries a hand *stall* or perhaps a head *stall*!

Hyperflite Skyhoundz World Finalist Paul West demonstrates a sequence of multiples during a back stall.

2007 Hyperflite Skyhoundz Open Division World Champion Danny Venegas demonstrates a back "stall."

More Stalls...

Hyperflite Skyhoundz World Finalist Ed Jakubowski gets his dog to jump up on his back for a "stall."

Hyperflite Skyhoundz World Finalist Tracy Custer prepares her canine for a leaping dismount from a "stall."

Canine Catches

Canine catches are always entertaining. They enjoyed a renaissance in the early 90's after World Champion *Gilbert's* routine included some radical new catch variations. You should be in good physical condition before you attempt to catch your canine. Ideally, you should catch your dog at that point in the air when it is floating in front of you with no momentum in any direction. That's the theory anyway. If the canine has momentum in any direction you risk back injuries. Common sense would dictate that a person of small stature probably shouldn't attempt to catch a canine of large stature. If your dog has an aversion to being held, then canine catches might not be in your best interest. As trainers, we have been nipped on a few occasions by surprised canines not expecting us to suddenly interrupt their flying sessions. So as not to frighten your pet, try having him jump into your arms when you are sitting on the sofa. Give a consistent command to your dog such as *arms* to alert him that you are about to catch him. Once your canine appears comfortable with the concept, you can try a basic catch. Position your dog a few steps away and hold the disc in the air as you might for the *leg over* discussed previously in this chapter. Give the *take* command and toss the disc in the air with the familiar *pizza toss* delivery. Try this a few times, at first, only touching your canine as he snags the disc in front of you. Then,

Peter Bloeme (Sequence)

1989 World Champion Jeff Perry goes both ways...he catches "Gilbert" in front of him...and behind his back! Then does it all

when the moment is right, say *arms* and cradle your canine in both arms. When you catch your dog, bend your knees slightly and be prepared to jog or walk with him in your arms to dissipate the energy of his momentum. A plethora of catch variations exist. Many are safe, and others are risky. With canine catches, trust is a bedrock concept. Don't drop your buddy!

LINK World Championship DVDs from years-gone-by feature video of some of the more unique and crowd pleasing catches performed by elite level competitors. These DVDs are available at the Skyhoundz store. http://skyhoundz.com/store.html

Tracy Custer catches her canine.

Jeff Hoot

over again with two discs!

Walt Mancini (Sequence)

Peter Bloeme tosses the disc to "Wizard" who then "taps" it back with his nose.

TAPPING

Tapping, or tipping as it is sometimes called, is a trick that has its roots in human disc competition where human freestylers tap the disc with feet, fingers, head and elbows. You don't see *tapping* much in canine competition because it is a counter-intuitive trick. That is to say, it is not instinctive for your canine to bounce a disc on its nose. When *tapping* is done well, it is greatly appreciated by judges and spectators alike. Since dogs naturally want to catch any disc in their vicinity, it takes quite a bit of doing, and even some trickery to get them to *tap,* rather than catch, a disc. To teach the *tap,* position your dog in front of you in a sitting or down position. Next, give the *tap* command and make an inverted toss at your canine's snout. If you make the toss so as to present the blunt top surface of the disc to your canine, it will be difficult for him to grab the disc in his mouth. The result is that the disc usually gets knocked back toward you. If this happens, catch the disc and reward your canine by saying *good tap.* You will likely have to practice tapping *ad nauseam* before your canine stops trying to catch the disc. It may also take a bit of work to get the timing and correct delivery angle down. If you get the trick dialed, you will be one of only a handful of disc doggers to perfect the trick. One challenging variation of the *tap* is the rarely seen *tap catch,* where the canine first taps the disc in the air, and then catches the disc before it hits the ground. *Wizard,* the 1984 World Champion, was the undisputed master of the *tap catch.*

A two-handed butterfly throw to an "over."

BUTTERFLY

As described previously in the Throwing Chapter, the butterfly throw (visualize a disc flying just like a *heads or tails* coin toss) is more easily caught by a canine if the disc rotates toward the dog's jaws. When attempting to teach the butterfly, keep the rotation of the disc on the slow side until your canine catches on. Once your canine is consistently catching the butterfly, you can accelerate the rate of rotation for effect. The butterfly throw can be made with a variety of deliveries. Use unique deliveries to distinguish yourself from the competition. As is the case with many throws, the butterfly toss can be used with *multiples*, *backflips*, *vaults*, and virtually any other trick you can imagine. In a sense, the butterfly is like a difficulty multiplier in that it renders any trick sequence in which it is featured, potentially higher scoring. A

World Champion Ron Ellis and "Maggy" demonstrate the

variation of the butterfly, called the *spinner* (the disc spins like a football instead of a coin toss) can also be employed to add some difficulty to a disc dog routine. *Spinner* throws work great with *over* tricks such as the leg *over*.

This sequence shows the tumbling action of a butterfly toss.

Jay Maldow

Peter Bloeme (Sequence)

butterfly sequence. Ellis flips the disc and Maggy makes the catch!

Jeff Hoot

Frank Montgomery demonstrates a challenging reverse butterfly throw in which the disc moves away from "Pixie Chick."

More Butterflies...

Here, the rotating butterfly has been tapped with another disc to set it spinning.

Hyperflite Skyhoundz World Finalist Dennis Alexander making a series of butterfly throws to his dog "Tango."

Sven Van Driessche (Sequence)

Sven Van Driessche

A butterfly throw can be made in many different ways. You can even kick the disc to put end-over-end spin on it.

VAULTING

Vaults are spectacular tricks that allow canines to achieve altitudes well beyond their normal jumping abilities. *Vaulting* canines achieve great heights by jumping off the thighs, back, or chest of their trainers. It is impossible not to notice how crowd pleasing *vaults* are. Canines soaring ten or more feet in the air are certainly a sight to behold. While the crowds may love them, it is worth noting that *vaults* are not a required element in competition. You can win a World Championship title without performing a single *vault*. Further, *vaults* are typically scored by technique and form — not height. So, if you must perform them, go long rather than high. Over the years we have seen *vaulting* canines that suffer, early in life, from joint and back problems. Disc dogs that were never *vaulted* may well continue to perform at a World Championship calibre at 11 and 12 years of age — long after their *vaulting* brethren have been sidelined. *Vaults* with a low trajectory are safest for your dog. You won't get any extra points in competition for launching your dog into the stratosphere and you may draw the ire of contest judges and your fellow competitors. Once more for emphasis: *vaults* are absolutely not necessary for competitive success! In fact, an interesting and innovative routine, sans *vaults*, is often a breath of fresh air to judges.

Although it might seem odd to advise against the performance of *vaults* and then teach you how to perform them, our philosophy is that a proper foundation in the trick is better than no foundation at all.

Sven Van Driessche (Sequence)

Jackie Parkin, Morgan Jarvis and "Blitz" demonstrate a "back vault" in Pairs Freestyle.

The simplest *vault* to teach is often referred to as the *leg vault* or *catapult*. It involves having your dog jump off your thigh like a springboard to catch the disc. For this *vault* you will need a heavy-duty neoprene thigh pad. Leg protection designed specifically for canine disc play is available through the Skyhoundz store. You may also be able to locate acceptable thigh protection at your local sporting goods store. You will find it easiest to teach (and later to perform) *vaults* from a standard starting position with consistent spacing between you and your canine. This will allow you to get your timing worked out and provide important consistency.

To teach the *leg vault*, your canine must first be comfortable jumping in close proximity to your body. If your ca-nine has issues with close contact, then you will need to employ a helper to teach this trick. Refer back to the section on teaching the *over* for some helpful tips. Once you have your canine positioned at an appropriate distance (close is better for the *leg vault*), stand sideways relative to your canine, lift the knee closest to your canine, and then place your foot just above the knee on your opposite leg. You will be standing on one foot when you do this so you may want to practice the stance a few times without your canine so as not to fall over and humiliate yourself in front of your furry comrade. When you've mastered the one-foot stance, hold the disc high above your thigh and give the *touch* command. During the course of jumping for the disc, your canine may touch or even push off

Long Photography, Inc. (Sequence)

Peter Bloeme and "Wizard" demonstrate the "catapult" or "thigh vault."

of your thigh. If he does, then say *good touch* and give him lots of praise. Touching will, after some practice, become full-fledged pushing off. As is probably obvious, *pushing off* is responsible for the great heights associated with *vaulting*.

If your dog continues to jump over your thigh without touching it, then congratulations are in order — you obviously have a great jumper! However, you will need to throttle him down a bit so he learns to push off, rather than jump over,

Jeff Hoot (Sequence)

It's always important to angle the disc properly so that your dog can easily make the catch.

"Side vault" combination.

your thigh. This is easy enough to accomplish. First, position your canine only a few feet from your leg so that he can't get a running start. Then, hold the disc a bit lower and further from your body but still in the direction of his travel. Now, slap the top of your thigh and give the *touch* command to initiate the *leg vault*. At this juncture, your goal should be to hold the disc in such a way as to cause your canine to touch, or push-off of, your thigh as he *takes* the disc from your hand.

Long Photography, Inc.

Chuck Middleton and "Flash" demonstrating a "chest vault" sequence.

When your dog is making consistent contact with your thigh, it's time to introduce a *vault* toss. The appropriate toss for a *leg vault* is a relatively flat, one-handed *pizza toss* with lots of spin. Be sure to put the disc in the air before your dog arrives at your thigh so that he can see his target before he pushes off to make the catch. It may take some practice to get your timing right but once you have it *dialed-in* the *leg vault* is a very consistently successful trick. If you have a small dog, or a weak jumper, you can perform the *leg vault* from a kneeling position.

Jeff Hoot (Sequence)

Mouth throw to a "back vault" combination.

A reverse "back vault" by John Casey and "Teagan."

Peter Bloeme

Back vaults and *chest vaults* get the biggest air and are most popular with trainers that do professional shows. To safely perform these *vaults* — neoprene rubber *vaulting* vests are required equipment. The *back vault* necessitates that you position your canine a little further away than you might with the *chest vault* and *leg vault*. Bend forward, at the waist, until you are comfortably positioned at a 45° or greater, angle. You can kneel on the ground, squat, or stand, but your goal should be to create a nice level platform for your canine to

Jeff Hoot

"Hip vault."

Jeff Perry

"Catapult" or "thigh vault."

launch from. At first, a helper may be necessary to help direct your canine, if he tries to run around, rather than over, your back. To initiate the *back vault* sequence, many competitors will reach over their own shoulders and slap the disc on their backs — the go signal for the canine. Contemporaneously (and we mean fast!) drop the disc low in front of you before launching the disc upward with a one-handed *pizza toss* delivery. The correct position for the disc to be in, when your canine reaches it, is a level attitude with lots of spin. Spin will give stability to the disc and keep it from wobbling or falling off to one side and thereby becoming difficult to catch. A common mistake made by beginners is to toss the disc upward at an uncatchable angle. If a sharply-angled disc is not in exactly the right spot, it will be nearly

impossible for your canine to grab because he will end up trying to grab the top surface of the disc rather than the rim of the disc. In most cases, the top surface of a disc is considerably larger than a canine's mouth. We refer to this type of throwing error as an *oblique presentation*. With such a throw, even though your timing is perfect, your dog is left staring — with open mouth — at a perfectly uncatchable disc.

Timing is everything with *vaults*. The most common reason for misses is late throws. Even top competitors get their timing out of whack from time-to-time. Timing problems happen most frequently with *back vaults* because we turn our backs on our canines while they sneakily creep an extra step closer than they should. It's not always obvious to the thrower that this is happen-

Jeff Perry

"Chest vault."

Jeff Perry

"Back vault."

Sven Van Driessche

Great timing and a flat "pizza toss" of the disc make it easier for your canine to complete a "vaulting" catch.

Jay Moldow

An "oblique presentation" is nearly impossible to catch.

ing, so have an experienced competitor observe your *vaulting* sequences if you think your timing might be off. In addition to misses, late throws drastically increase the possibility of injury because canines, in an effort to catch your late throws, will twist while airborne in ways that set them up for bad landings. The whole point of getting the disc in the air before the push-off is to give your canine an opportunity to adjust before he pushes off of you.

Remember, if you must *vault* your canine, train with an expert disc dogger and practice the *vaulting* stances and throws until you have them perfected. Temper your enthusiasm for ultra-high *vaults* with concern for the welfare of your best friend. Our fondest wish is for you and your canine companion to enjoy disc sports for many years to come.

2005 Hyperflite Skyhoundz Open Division World Champion Tony Hoard demonstrates a kneeling "chest vault." Through this series of photographs you can see that the disc is upside-down, a more challenging delivery.

PRO TIP

Competition is great, but don't lose sight of why you started throwing discs to your best friend in the first place. A couple of years ago, I caught myself being too competitive, and my dog "Bowditch" and I just weren't having as much fun as we used to have. It affected our performance and morale. I learned that sometimes you have to leave the measuring tape, cones and stopwatch at home. Grab a disc, walk over to your favorite field, and just play. When I remember to stop thinking about competition and start having fun, throwing to "Bowditch" is a total blast. He never fails to bring a smile to my face every time he snags that disc out of the air.

— *Larry Beatty and "Bowditch," 2004 Hyperflite*

More Vaults...

Two different ways of attempting a Pairs Freestyle "back vault."

1991 World Champion Ron Ellis and his dog "Maggy" demonstrate a "catapult vault" in both directions.

MicroDogs can enjoy "vaulting" as much as the big dogs!

Todd Duncan and "K2," 2004 Skyhoundz MicroDog World Champions

The modern disc dog competition circuit is a cornucopia of events held in locations around the globe. The Hyperflite Skyhoundz World Canine Disc Championship Series, the world's largest, features more than 150 canine disc competitions worldwide.

However, we would be remiss if we neglected to mention that the Skyhoundz Series is not the only game in town. Many fine contest series exist that are staged by dedicated individuals and organizations who pour their hearts and souls into events that have well-developed followings of loyal enthusiasts.

These competition series are listed in alphabetical order:

Ashley Whippet Invitational (AWI) — Features a combined freestyle and mini-distance event.

Flying Disc Dog Open (FDDO) — Features freestyle, distance, speed disc and obstacle course events.

The International Disc Dog Handlers' Association (IDDHA) — Features distance, freestyle, and single-disc format events.

The Quadruped — Features a canine long distance event.

U.S. Disc Dog Nationals (USDDN) — Features freestyle and toss and fetch events.

UFO — Features freestyle, throw and catch and longshot events.

Believe it or not, the judges always want you to do the best you can. It makes judging more fun.

Walt Mancini

Competition has changed greatly since its beginnings in 1974 at the Rose Bowl.

For links to the myriad competition series mentioned previously, as well as new events that pop up from time-to-time, visit: http://hyperflite.com/ discdogcompetitions.html

Most of the competitive formats available to disc doggers share similar attributes, but there are enough differences to keep things interesting. Regardless of the competition format that you ultimately decide is best for you, it is important that you support those contest organizers that devote considerable time and effort toward creating fun events for you and your canine. Our view is that the community of disc dog enthusiasts is strengthened by a vibrant and collaborative group of organizers all trying to be just a little bit different than one another. And, let's not forget the disc dog clubs. These geographic nuclear families of disc doggers are the spokes that keep the disc dog wheel turning. If you want to truly experience the disc dog lifestyle, then join a club near you.

For links to disc dog clubs visit: http://hyperflite.com/ discdogclubs.html

SPORTSMANSHIP

Polls have shown that the primary reason that people participate in canine disc competitions is because their dogs love it. Regardless of how you finish in competition, you will always be a winner in your dog's eyes. Sometimes we lose sight of that simple fact as we become more experienced and more active on the competition circuit. Winning and losing, in canine disc competitions, should always be secondary to the special relationship you have with your canine. You are unquestionably your dog's hero when you take the time to play and have fun together. Winning or losing is simply

Competition isn't just for the young dogs. Canadians Dennis Alexander and his German Shepherd "Tango" competed at the Hyperflite Skyhoundz World Championship several times before her retirement from the competitive circuit.

Jeff Perry

Sven Van Driessche

Competitors compete in disc dog events for the fun and camaraderie rather than for large prizes.

not something that matters to canines. We could all learn from their example.

Competition organizers and officials strive to make disc dog competitions a fun and challenging activity for both human and canine alike. Competitions are also a great way to meet other people who love their canines. Unlike most canine sports, disc dog play requires of its participants — both human and canine — the same measure of dedication, skill and effort. But no matter how competitive you are, your canine will love you just as much even if every throw you make isn't perfect and even if that big trophy doesn't find its way to your mantle.

Regardless of how much you prepare, or how hard you try, sooner or later you or your canine teammate will have a bad day on the playing field. On those less

than magical days, you may be irritated or disappointed in your performance, or your luck, or even your scores.

While it is natural for a competitor to try his or her best and strive to win, it is important to be mindful of why you got involved with the sport in the first place. If you are like most people, you probably were attracted to canine disc sports because there is no better way to have fun with your dog and no activity that your dog will enjoy more.

On occasion, there may be a temptation to blame competition judges when we fail to achieve our goals. Often, with calm reflection, we can analyze our performances objectively, discover our own failings, learn from them, and move on. Not only is judging extremely difficult, it is also a subjective endeavor. No matter how hard contest organizers try to eliminate the subjective element in judging, in the end, human beings are involved in the process and this means that the scores that human judges give you may not be the scores that you or your posse of friends believe you should have received. All parents think their kids are perfect and all dog owners think their dogs are perfect. And, of course, everyone is right. But some people are more right than others and that difficult determination is left to the judges.

Unfortunately, there have been epi-sodes of poor sportsmanship at, or after, canine disc competitions. Although you may be tempted to unload on the judges after a competition, this approach will never yield a positive outcome. Typically, confrontation ends the possibility of dialogue with the judge because judges are less likely to offer constructive suggestions on improving a routine to someone who is attacking them because they disagree with the outcome.

No one enjoys seeing athletes displaying poor sportsmanship and a disc

GRAVY

The Accidental Champion — *"Mastodon," or "Donnie" for short, was an accident. Two dogs that weren't supposed to breed, did. And one little puppy that wasn't supposed to live, did. "Donnie" the accidental puppy, then left our household for new homes on two different occasions, but when things didn't work out, he found his way back to us. To his credit, "Donnie" bonded with my wife Lisa, allowing her to experience for the first time that unique emotion that follows when you realize that your dog loves you unconditionally and asks for nothing in return.*

Although "Donnie" was a lover, he wasn't much of a disc dog. Even at three years of age he demonstrated virtually no desire to catch anything other than long throws. Then, strangely, around his fourth birthday, "Donnie" suddenly developed some coordination. With coordination came a greater desire to catch the close-in tosses.

It was about that same time that a former World Champion saw "Donnie" play and made a fateful comment, You need to work with him. He has a lot of potential! I chuckled at the thought, but the seed was planted. So, after months of work I finally entered "Donnie" in his first freestyle competition. Our performance was utterly dreadful. For the first time in 14 years I failed to make the cut at the Regional finals. I was so disappointed that I vowed that we would work hard to make sure it didn't happen again.

Fast forward two years and there "Donnie" was — basking in the limelight of World Championship titles in both the Open and Sport Divisions of the 2002 Hyperflite Skyhoundz World Canine Disc Championship.

Looking back, I might have guessed that "Donnie" would capture our hearts because dogs have a way of doing that to us. But, I would never have guessed that "Donnie", the accidental puppy, would go on to win the affection and admiration of so many disc dog fans that saw his effortless grace and athleticism.

— Chuck Middleton, 2002 Hyperflite Skyhoundz Open and Sport Division
World Champion, Skyhoundz Lifetime Achievement Award Recipient

dog competition is a family-oriented event, with children and sensitive animals present. It is not the place for heated confrontations, unseemly displays, or boisterous challenges of officials.

Whether or not you agree with a judge's determination, there is nothing that can be done to alter the final result. A better approach is to visit with the judge after the competition and ask for guidance or tips for improving your scores for a future competition. Once you see how the judge evaluated your performance, you can make the changes necessary to ensure success in the future. Remember, these same judges may be judging you in a future competition and doing it your way will probably not increase your chances of competitive success.

Judging, for those brave enough to do it, is a thankless job. It's the least appreciated, yet most difficult role in the

Sven Van Driessche

Judging can be a thankless job.

PRO TIP

Practice Makes Perfect — *Our canines give 100% every time we play disc with them. We owe it to them to be on our game as well. Practice! Practice! Practice!*

Whether you compete or just play in your yard, you've probably noticed that we humans seem to make more mistakes throwing the disc than our canines do catching them. Whether you've been playing for years or are just starting out, you'll know that you've made a less than perfect throw the first time your canine looks back at you with a — What was that? — look.

Think of your canine as a highly-trained athlete. Canine athletes need rest just as human athletes do. After a hard day of disc play, or a long competition, give your canine some rest. Rest days create the perfect opportunity for you to practice your throwing. Take a stack of discs to wherever you play and practice making perfect throws. Set up some cones, put a ribbon around a tree, or baseball backstop, to give you something to aim for. Try different grips on the disc, work on your stance, and let the discs fly. See what works best for you. You'll both be amazed at how quickly you will improve and you'll both have a lot more fun when you play together! Most importantly, don't become discouraged, your next stop might be the Skyhoundz World Championship!

— John Bilheimer, 2006 Hyperflite Skyhoundz
Sport Division World Champion

sport. Take a moment, the next time you compete, to thank the judges for their sacrifice and hard work. This simple act, heard so rarely by judges, can make it all seem worthwhile.

CANINE WELFARE

- Competitors are responsible for the safety and welfare of their dogs. Competing canines must be supervised and under the care and control of their throwers/owners at all times. Only the competing dog, thrower and contest officials are allowed on the field during competition. Dogs must be leashed at all times, except when competing.

- There are presently no limitations as to the number of events you or your dog may enter, or in which divisions. However, the same thrower/dog combination may only compete once per

division/class. It is the owner/trainer's responsibility to ensure that competing canines do not compete in more events than would be advisable given the prevailing weather conditions, with specific consideration given to the fitness and general health of the competing canine. At Hyperflite Skyhoundz Regional Qualifiers, Open Qualifiers, International Qualifiers, and the World Championship, the Chief Judge will have final authority on the issue of whether a dog is fit to compete.

- Abusive treatment of a canine, or any conduct of a competitor which might be perceived by spectators as such, will not be tolerated. Contest officials may disqualify any competitor who engages in this type of behav-

The Hyperflite Skyhoundz World Championship boasts some pretty impressive hardware for the winners.

Sven Van Driessche

Sven Van Driessche (Sequence)

He sees it, he tracks it, he closes in for the "kill." No plastic left behind with this dog.

ior. The wearing of electronic or chemical training aids, of any sort (active or inactive), will not be permitted during competition.

● Competitors with overly aggressive dogs may not be permitted to compete if such canines are believed to pose a danger to people or other canines.

● Freestyle *vaults*, utilizing the trainer's body as a launch pad, should be minimized or excluded from routines altogether. If attempted, *vaults* should be performed in a controlled and safe manner. Excessive height, or frequent repetitions of *vaults*, will not increase the likelihood of a higher score.

GENERAL COMPETITION RULES

● Each contestant must read and sign, without modification, the Hyperflite Skyhoundz Registration Form, which contains a liability waiver and publicity release. Competitors are responsible for reading and understanding the competition rules before they compete.

FACT

Most people know that dogs use their tongues like radiators to stay cool on hot days. But did you also know that dogs sweat through the pads of their feet? If your dog is panting heavily on a hot day, pour cool water on the pads of your canine's feet to help cool him off. You might also try having your panting pooch stand on a cool wet towel.

- Because of time constraints, no practice throws will be permitted at any Hyperflite Skyhoundz events.

- No props of any kind, including capes, vests or other adornments worn by canines, are permitted in competition.

- Female dogs in any stage of heat will not be permitted to compete and must not be brought to the competition site.

- Dog owners/trainers are required to clean up after their dog's nature breaks. If a nature break takes place during any event, time will be suspended until the break has concluded. During a nature break, a thrower should maintain his or her position on the field and should not attempt to gather discs or move closer to the competing canine while time is suspended. Time will resume at the conclusion of the nature break. Any clean-up necessary must be done by the thrower upon completion of the round.

- Where required by local ordinance, all participating dogs must have proof of Rabies inoculation and license. Parvo and Kennel Cough vaccinations are strongly recommended.

- If a spectator's dog runs onto the field during a competitor's round, time will be suspended. Once the spectator's dog is leashed and has been removed from the field, time will resume from the point of interruption. Officials will use every effort to

Sven Van Driessche

An example of "too many judges." Competitors attempt some good-natured judging during the authors' charity Pairs Freestyle exhibition. Just don't read the scores!

allow the interrupted team to be returned to their status on the field, including physical field location and time remaining, at the point of the interruption.

● The Hyperflite Skyhoundz Championship Series represents family entertainment at its finest. Accordingly, competitors should avoid confrontations with other competitors or challenges of contest officials. Abusive language or other inappropriate or unsportsmanlike behavior may result in a contestant's disqualification from competition.

Only those Hyperflite Skyhoundz Local Championships, U.S. Regional Qualifiers, Open Qualifiers, International Qualifiers and the World Championship listed in the Hyperflite Skyhoundz schedule http://skyhoundz.com are officially sanctioned by Skyhoundz. Skyhoundz Officials reserve the right to change format, competition rules, time allotments, etc. at all levels of competition.

COMPETITION DISCS

Skyhoundz has selected Hyperflite flying discs as the official flying discs of the Hyperflite Skyhoundz World Canine Disc Championship Series. At all Hyperflite DiscDogathons and at Skyhoundz Locals, Regional Qualifiers, Open Qualifiers, International Qualifiers, and the World Championship, competitors may, in their sole discretion, elect to use Hyperflite discs of any size or weight or the safe solid plastic canine discs of the manufacturer of their choice. Discs from different manufacturers and of different sizes and weights may also be mixed and matched in the discretion of each competitor. However, competitors entering the MicroDog Division at any Hyperflite Skyhoundz competition, must use the K-10 Pup, (Competition Standard Pup, FrostBite Pup, Jawz Pup, or SofFlite Pup disc) or a similar or smaller-sized solid plastic canine disc made by another manufacturer. Also, in Hyperflite Xtreme Distance events, due to national and world record considerations, the Hyperflite Competition Standard disc, Wham-O standard Fastback Frisbee disc, or Hero standard disc shall be used exclusively.

At all Hyperflite Skyhoundz competitions, one Hyperflite disc will be given to each competitor. Competitors are responsible for supplying any additional discs they will need for competition.

SKYHOUNDZ SERIES OVERVIEW

The Hyperflite Skyhoundz World Canine disc Championship Series consists of Local Championships, U.S. Regional Qualifiers, Open Qualifiers, an ever growing number of International Qualifiers, and the World Championship.

Hyperflite's sponsorship of the Skyhoundz Series ensures that disc dog competitors, worldwide, will have exciting venues in which to compete.

It's helpful to practice your Freestyle routine without your dog to make sure you remember all the moves without tiring your dog out. Here Peter and Carolyn Williams work through a sequence in their Pairs Freestyle routine without their dog.

Sven Van Driessche (Sequence)

And, here you can see the move Peter and Carolyn Williams were practicing earlier as it appears in competition.

Sven Van Driessche

Peter Bloeme

Lpmg ljptbgralju Omd

Dogs can be hams and showmen too...."Look ma, no paws or jaws."

A good "Presentation" score requires that you get involved in the action.

Local Championships Hyperflite Skyhoundz Local Championships are free events, open to all competitors regardless of experience. You are welcome to enter as many Hyperflite Skyhoundz Local Championships as you like.

Regional Qualifiers At Hyperflite Skyhoundz Regional Qualifiers, top-finishing teams qualify for invitations to the World Championship. Eligibility is based solely on residence in a geographic region. See map on page 245. Registration fees apply.

Open Qualifiers At Hyperflite Skyhoundz Open Qualifiers, top-finishing teams qualify for invitations to the World Championship. Anyone may compete in the Open Qualifiers and there are no geographic limitations for competitor entry. Even current World Finalists may compete and attempt to earn additional invitations to the World Championship. In addition, international competitors are also eligible to compete in Open Qualifiers. Registration fees apply.

International Qualifiers International Qualifiers for the Hyperflite Skyhoundz World Championship are held in a number of countries. Competitors from Canada are eligible to compete in any Hyperflite Skyhoundz Qualifier held in Canada. Competitors from any European country may compete in any Hyperflite Skyhoundz Qualifier held in Europe. Competitors from Asian countries may compete in any International Qualifier held in any Asian country. U.S. residents are not eligible to earn invitations to the World Championship at an International Qualifier, but may compete for awards. Registration fees apply.

World Championship The Hyperflite Skyhoundz World Canine Disc Championship is the premier event in canine sports. Competitors qualify for the World Championship through Regional, Open, and International Qualifiers. Each year, the World Championship is held in a host city in the U.S. Partici-

Susan Jones tosses a "Jawz Pup disc" to "Whoopin' Roo."

pation in the World Championship is always free to those who qualify.

HYPERFLITE SERIES OVERVIEW

Hyperflite DiscDogathons Hyperflite DiscDogathons are staged by dog and disc clubs and other similar volunteer organizations and are open to all competitors regardless of experience. Competitors are welcome to enter as many Hyperflite DiscDogathons as they like and there are no geographic restrictions. Registration fees may apply.

Hyperflite Xtreme Distance Challenge Hyperflite Xtreme Distance Challenge events are typically stand-alone events that showcase the long distance catching abilities of competing teams. Participation is open to all competitors regardless of experience. Teams compete in Men's and Women's Divisions in several classes determined by the weight of the flying discs being used. Competitors are welcome to enter as many Hyperflite Xtreme Distance Challenge events as they like and there

are no geographic restrictions. Registration fees may apply.

SKYHOUNDZ EVENT RULES

Distance/Accuracy Distance/Accuracy is a fast-paced event in which teams attempt to score points by completing

The barracuda strikes!

Sven Van Driessche (Sequence)

Distance/Accuracy sequence of disc dog tracking, running down, and making the catch inbounds.

as many catches as possible within various scoring zones in the time allotted.

Distance/Accuracy competitors are allowed 60 seconds and one disc to score as many points as possible. If, during the round a competitor believes the disc has become unsafe (e.g.: broken rim, or a large tear in the disc), it may be handed to the line judge for replacement (if the competitor has provided such a replacement). Time will not be suspended during a disc change. Notification of time remaining will be uniform for all competitors: 30 seconds, 10 sec-

onds, and a countdown of the final five seconds before time is called.

The Distance/Accuracy field set-up provides the ability for individual competitors to throw in either direction, however, competitors cannot change throwing direction once time has begun. Field dimensions and the ability to throw from either end are subject to change, at the discretion of contest officials, due to overall field limitations or for safety considerations.

The thrower and canine are required to be behind the throwing line

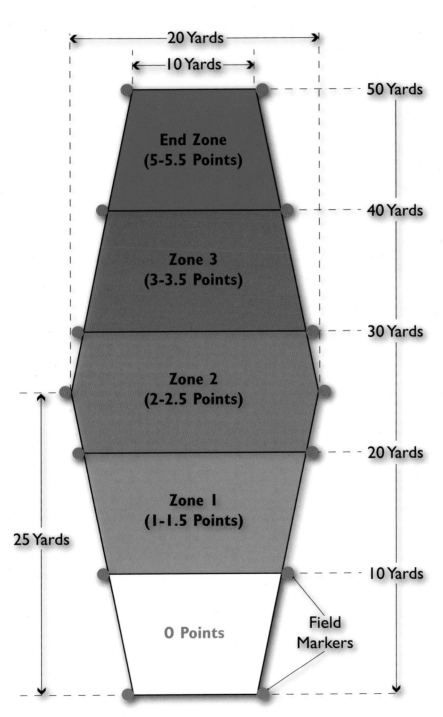

Distance/Accuracy Field Layout

Thom Gillott

I would clap for those amazing disc dogs, if I could!

in the lower scoring zone. If a canine tips the disc and subsequently catches the disc inbounds, the catch will be scored where the catch was completed.

Scoring is based on the following point scale. No points are awarded for catches under 10 yards.

Zone 1	(10-20 yards)	1 Point
Zone 2	(20-30 yards)	2 Points
Zone 3	(30-40 yards)	3 Points
End Zone	(40-50 yards)	5 Points

An additional half-point bonus will be awarded for each successful catch in which the dog makes a catch with all paws clearly off the ground in an obvious jumping effort and subsequently lands with all paws in a scoring zone.

Distance/Accuracy Tie-Breaker If there is a tie for first, second or third place, the tie will be broken by the following criteria, as necessary: 1) The competitor with the fewest throws in both rounds, 2) A Face-off round with each team receiving one Distance/Accuracy throw.

The dog making the higher scoring catch will be declared the victor. If the teams are still tied after each has made one throw, Face-off continues until one dog makes a higher scoring catch than the other. Officials will permit the competitors to rest their dogs as necessary.

Freestyle Freestyle is a free-form, choreographed, routine scored by judges with an emphasis on success, variety, innovation, and the athletic skills of the canine and thrower.

Teams competing in Freestyle will receive a maximum of 90 seconds per round (120 seconds at the World Championship). Routines must last at least 60 seconds (90 seconds at the World Championship) to be scored. Competitors in Freestyle are permitted to use up to five discs. Timing begins when the

before time starts. When the competitor is ready, the line judge will signal the announcer by raising an arm. Soon after, a start cue will be given by the announcer indicating that time has begun. If, in the opinion of the line judge, the dog leaves before time begins, time will be reset to zero and a restart will be initiated. Competitors may send their canines downfield, or throw, anytime after the start signal is sounded.

The thrower must always throw from behind the throwing line and between the throwing line cones, but may move freely around the field at other times. A throw will not be scored if the thrower steps on or over the throwing line prior to or during the release of the disc (foot fault). If the disc leaves the thrower's hand before time is called, the throw will be scored if caught by the canine inbounds.

To receive points, catches must be completed by a canine with all paws landing within one of the official scoring zones. If a canine catches a disc with paws in more than one scoring zone, the catch will be scored as if it were made

"Out" is the Distance/Accuracy call!
The judges have to make the tough calls.

DISCS

Sven Van Driessche

Canine Freestyle requires that both human and canine work together as a team.

disc is placed in flight, or the canine attempts to catch or pick-up a disc placed on the ground, or takes the disc from any part of a thrower's or canine's body. Countdown of time remaining will be uniform for all competitors: 60 seconds, 30 seconds, 10 seconds and time.

Contestants who bring their own music should present it to contest officials when called to the on-deck area. Music should be on a CD (compact disc) that is marked with the competitor's name and desired track number. This information should also be noted on the outside of the CD case. Contestants must choose music that is suitable for a family audience.

Judges will disregard tricks that do not begin or conclude with a disc in flight except roller throws. Takes — moves in which a disc is handed off to the dog — will not be scored.

PAWS FREESTYLE SCORING SYSTEM

Competing teams will receive scores ranging from 1-10, in half-point increments, for each of the following four categories:

Presentation The team's presentation of a crowd-pleasing routine with exciting choreography, continuous flow, good disc management and smooth transitions.

Athleticism Intensity and athleticism in completing catches, tricks or maneuvers together with a dog's speed, quickness, leaping ability relative to its size and control over his/her body while competing.

Wow!Factor Ability to successfully complete challenging tricks or moves, including successful catches of throws with varied spins or releases. Also, the presentation of completely new moves, or a novel or unique presentation of a previously performed move, will result in higher scores in this category.

Success The team's ability to successfully execute a routine with specific consideration given for the difficulty of the throws, catches and tricks.

Under the PAWS scoring system, judges will evaluate each team's ability to cleanly execute a challenging, varied and exciting routine within the time allotted. Although there are specific categories that focus on execution (Success) and difficulty (Wow!Factor), a failure to score well in either of these categories may impact a competitor's scores in all of the PAWS categories. This is because the judges must account for differences between the routines of the competi-

tors that are competing on a given day.

For example, even if two competitors have perfect rounds they will not necessarily each receive a score of 10 in the Success category. Instead, the more difficult routine will typically receive a higher score in Success than the simpler routine. Similarly, if two competitors have equally difficult rounds, it is likely that the competitor with fewer misses will receive the higher score in the Wow!Factor category.

Vaults, utilizing the trainer's body as a launch pad, should be minimized or excluded from routines altogether. If attempted, *vaults* should be performed in a controlled and safe manner. Excessive

Here is a great example of "Athleticism." The dog is jumping over his trainer (not a "vault") to make the catch.

Peter Bloeme

height, or frequent repetition of *vaults*, will not increase the likelihood of a higher score. *Vaults* are not required for success in Hyperflite Skyhoundz competitions. A *vault* is to be valued no differently than any other trick of similar difficulty. Many World Championship titles have been won with *vault*-free routines or with *vaults* minimized.

Freestyle Tie-Breaker If there is a tie for first, second, or third place, the tie will be broken by the following criteria, as necessary: 1) The team with the highest combined scores in the Athleticism and Wow!Factor categories, 2) A Snapshot round will take place with each team alternating turns and receiving ten seconds in which to demonstrate their strongest trick or cluster of tricks. Order of competition will be determined by a coin toss. The timekeeper will announce the

start of Snapshot when each competitor signals his or her readiness to begin. The judges will then declare a winner based on their impressions of the overall quality of the Snapshot performances.

Pairs Freestyle As the name implies, Pairs Freestyle is essentially choreographed Freestyle employing two throwers and one canine.

With the safety of the canine always in mind, Pairs Freestyle teams demonstrate interesting variations on multiples, simultaneous throws, cross-feeding (i.e., alternating) throws to a canine, etc. Always exciting to watch, Pairs Freestyle offers endless possibilities for innovation and teamwork and doubles the fun for competing canines.

We believe that Pairs Freestyle is safer than an event in which two teams, each with a canine, are simultaneously work-

Sven Van Driessche (Sequence)

Innovative "foot stall" in Pairs Freestyle.

ing on a field. It has been our experience that canines, especially in the hands of inexperienced novice teams, are injured this way in greater frequency than in any other disc related activity. With Pairs Freestyle, the possibility of a canine-to-canine entanglement is eliminated.

That said, even though an additional thrower is involved, Pairs Freestyle routines should feature the substantial involvement of the canine. In other words, the judges are looking for routines that aren't merely human Freestyle routines with an occasional throw to the canine team member.

Throwing from human-to-human, though regarded as a transfer, could potentially impact the various applicable scoring categories. In other words, if a transfer is executed cleanly and adds to the routine, it could positively impact a team's score. A miss might have the opposite impact. Although transfers not involving the competing canine certainly could be an interesting and exciting component of a pairs routine, human-to-human throwing interaction should be balanced so as to highlight the significant involvement of the canine. Always, the emphasis will be on the canine.

In Pairs Freestyle, all the same rules for Freestyle apply with two exceptions. Competitors are allowed up to 10 discs and the category Teamwork (1-10 points) is added to the PAWS Freestyle scoring categories.

Teamwork Teamwork takes into consideration the relationship, choreography, field use, and fluidity of movement of the team during the routine.

Pairs Freestyle Tie-Breaker If there is a tie for first, or second place, the tie will be broken by the following criteria, as necessary: 1) The team with the highest

Sven Van Driessche (Sequence)

Team Time Trial or Team Distance/Accuracy requires competitors to alternate throwers.

combined scores in the Athleticism and Wow!Factor categories from the Free-style Round(s), 2) A Snapshot round will take place with each team alternating turns and receiving ten seconds in which to demonstrate their strongest trick or cluster of tricks. Order of competition will be determined by a coin toss. The timekeeper will announce the start of Snapshot when each competitor signals his or her readiness to begin. The judges will then declare a winner based on their impressions of the overall quality of the Snapshot performances.

Time Trial In Time Trial, each competitor or team will attempt to complete two 20-yard throws to a canine in the shortest amount of time possible. To qualify as a successful throw, the disc must be caught by the canine beyond the 20-yard line that runs from one side of the field to the other (there are no side-boundary lines). A maximum time of one minute will be permitted.

The thrower and canine are required to be behind the throwing line before time starts. When the competitor is ready, the line judge (with a stopwatch) will say *Go!* indicating that time has begun. If, in the opinion of the line judge, the dog leaves before time begins, time will be reset to zero and a restart will be initiated. Competitors may send their canines downfield, or throw, anytime after the start signal is sounded.

The thrower must remain behind the throwing line for all throws, but may move freely around the field at other times. A throw will not count if the thrower steps on or over the throwing line prior to or during the release of the disc.

At least two throws must be successfully completed (past the 20-yard mark) in order for a team to avoid being scored *Did Not Finish* (DNF). Time will stop when the canine crosses back over the start/finish line in possession of the disc after completing the required two 20-yard catches. However, if, after two successful catches, the canine drops the disc in front of the finish line, the thrower may retrieve the disc and time will stop when the thrower and canine cross the finish line regardless of who is in actual possession of the disc. The fastest canine/thrower team with two successful catches wins.

If a team's round is interrupted, by a loose canine on the playing field, the team will be permitted to restart the round. Time will not be suspended during nature breaks.

DISCDOGATHON EVENT RULES

The Hyperflite DiscDogathon host organization may choose from a menu of seven competition events and may also add their own *Club Choice* event. Hyperflite DiscDogathon host organizations custom tailor their events to serve the needs of the competitors who will be attending.

Hyperflite DiscDogathons may, in the discretion of the host organization, take place over two days and encompass all of the following events: Boomerang, Bullseye, Distance/Accuracy, Extreme Distance, Freestyle, Spot Landing, Time Trial, and Club Choice events.

PRO TIP

Disc Management — Good pool players never make a shot without knowing where the cue ball will end up when it stops rolling. Good disc management skills are a bit like that because, when you make your tosses, you should know exactly where the dog will catch the discs and where the two of you will come together on the field after each series of tricks or catches. If you map out your routine properly, and practice until the two of you can do it in your sleep, an amazing thing happens. Your dog begins to trust you to make consistently good throws and you begin to trust your dog to catch your throws. Suddenly, you can make tosses without watching to see what happens. This frees you to gather up discs and focus on getting ready for the next set of moves. To contest judges, your routine will appear to have a fluid quality that sets it apart from other routines.

Even though your routine may run like a well-oiled machine, the dog element of your machine will still appreciate a kiss and pat on the head as you leave the playing field.

—Todd Duncan, 2006 Hyperflite Skyhoundz MicroDog World Champion

Sven Van Driessche (Sequence)

Originality, as in this body roll, in Freestyle keeps the sport interesting and the judges entertained.

mum amount of time. Many competitors find a boomerang-like trajectory to be most effective, hence the name Boomerang. Time begins when the disc leaves the throwers hand and ends when the disc is first touched by the competing canine. The throw must be caught before touching the ground to be scored. The longest time between the throw and catch determines the winner. Canine and thrower must be within the designated throwing circle at the time a throw is made. A canine may be restrained by another helper, if necessary, to prevent false starts. The longest time of three attempts will be scored.

Boomerang field set-up: A large open, flat, grassy area free of obstacles with a 4-yard diameter throwing circle.

Boomerang Tie-Breaker If there is a tie for first, second or third place, the tie will be broken by alternating Boomerang throws between the tied teams until one team achieves a winning time. Officials will permit the teams to rest their dogs as necessary.

Bullseye is a fast-paced and updated derivation of the original circular canine disc distance format. Scoring rings are located at 8 and 15 yards, respectively, from the throwing circle. Competitors may use two discs to complete throws in any direction. The thrower and the canine must be within a 4-yard (in diameter) circle for the first throw. Thereafter, the thrower must be within the throwing circle at the time each throw is made. Competitors receive one minute to score as many points as they can. One point is awarded for catches made between the 8 and 15-yard lines, and two points are awarded for throws out-

Boomerang Competitors are given up to three attempts to achieve a successful catch with the goal being to throw the disc in such a manner as to keep the disc in the air for the maxi-

side of the 15-yard line. An extra point is awarded for each catch made by a canine with all paws off the ground.

Bullseye field set-up: An open, flat, grassy area free of obstacles with concentric 4, 8, and 15-yard diameter circles.

Bullseye Tie-Breaker If there is a tie for first, second or third place, the tie will be broken by the following criteria, as necessary: 1) The team with the fewest total throws, 2) A Face-off round with each team receiving one Bullseye throw. The dog making the higher scoring catch will be declared the victor. If the teams are still tied after each has made one throw, Face-off continues until one dog makes a higher scoring catch than the other. Officials will permit the competitors to rest their dogs as necessary.

Distance/Accuracy is a fast-paced event in which teams attempt to score points by completing as many catches as possible within various scoring zones within the time allotted. Rules set forth on pages 225-228 apply.

Extreme Distance is a pure distance event. Canines must not cross the throwing line until the disc leaves the thrower's hand. The thrower may not step on or over the line at the time of the throw. A canine may be restrained with the aid of a helper if desired. Catches will be measured from the start line to the point where the rear-most paw of the canine contacts the ground at the time of the catch. Successful tipped catches will be counted as being caught at the point where the canine first made contact with the disc regardless of the point that the canine actually becomes in full possession of the disc.

Due to national and world record considerations, the Hyperflite Competition Standard disc, Wham-O standard Fastback Frisbee disc, or Hero standard disc must be used. Competitors receive 90 seconds in which to make as many attempts as they wish. Competitors may change discs between throws. If the disc leaves the throwers hand before time is called, it will be scored.

"Sparky" competed successfully against the big dogs many years before the MicroDog Division was created.

Peter Bloeme

Open Qualifier shot from the air shows competitor tents and the Distance/Accuracy field.

Freestyle The Freestyle rules set forth on pages 228-232 apply, however, teams competing in Freestyle will receive a maximum of 2 minutes (120 seconds) per round. Routines must run at least 90 seconds to be scored.

Freestyle Tie-Breaker If there is a tie for first, second or third place, the tie will be broken by the following criteria, as necessary: 1) The team with the highest combined scores in the Athleticism and Wow!Factor categories, 2) A Snapshot round will take place with each team alternating turns and receiving ten seconds in which to demonstrate their strongest trick or cluster of tricks. Order of competition will be determined by a coin toss. The timekeeper will announce the start of Snapshot when each competitor signals his or her readiness to begin. The judges will then declare a winner based on their impressions of the overall quality of the Snapshot performances.

Spot Landing allows the local host to configure circular landing zones in different locations on the competition field. Competitors are rewarded with various point values for catches in which the canine lands with all paws inside a scoring zone. The Hyperflite DiscDogathon host determines the point values, location and distances of landing zones from the throwing area. Catches landing outside scoring zones are worth one point each (canine effort point(s), however, the thrower must attempt to reach the scoring areas to earn the canine effort point(s). Competitors receive 60 seconds to score as many points as they can.

Spot Landing Tie-Breaker If there is a tie for first, second or third place, the tie will be broken by the following criteria, as necessary: 1) The team with the fewest total throws, 2) A Face-off round with each team receiving one Spot Landing throw. The team making the higher scoring catch will be declared the victor. If the teams are still tied after each has made one throw, Face-off continues until one dog makes a higher scoring catch than the other. Officials will permit the competitors to rest their dogs as necessary.

 TimeTrial Each team will attempt to complete two 20-yard throws in the shortest amount of time as described more fully on pages 234-235.

 Club Choice is an event to be determined by and judged in accordance with the rules established by the Hyperflite DiscDogathon host organization.

Hyperflite Xtreme Distance Challenge

XDC FOR CANINES!

HYPERFLITE XTREME DISTANCE CHALLENGE EVENT RULES

Hyperflite's Xtreme Distance Challenge (Hyperflite XDC) gives canines exactly what they want — insanely long throws. Hyperflite XDC's are stand-alone events meant to showcase the pure speed and catching ability of canines and the throwing skills of the human team member. Teams compete in two divisions (Men's and Women's) in three distinct classes (Light Plastic, Classic Plastic, and Unlimited Plastic). All teams compete in two 90-second rounds

A nice butterfly delivery.

Peter Bloeme

(as many throws as a team can make within the 90-second throwing period). The top three teams in both divisions of all three classes (18 total teams) advance to a final face-off round. These top teams, by virtue of their previous long distance throws, compete in a final face-off round to try and improve upon their previous distances. Throws from both preliminary rounds, as well as the face-off round, are reviewed to determine the longest throws of the day. Awards are given to the three teams posting the longest throw in each division and class (i.e., Men's Light Plastic, Men's Classic Plastic, Men's Unlimited Plastic, Women's Light Plastic, Women's Classic Plastic, and Women's Unlimited Plastic). Entry fees apply. All proceeds from Hyperflite XDCs benefit the contest host organizations.

The recommended minimum field set-up for Xtreme Distance is a flat, grassy rectangular area, 50 yards x 110 yards, that is free of obstructions. The location of the throwing line will be dictated by the field geography and wind direction. Once the throwing line is determined it will remain the same for all competitors throughout the round. The contest host may change the throwing direction only after all competitors have completed a round.

On-deck teams, when called must immediately proceed from the staging area, to the throwing area. Once the team arrives in the throwing area, a *prepare to throw* 15-second warning will be given. Thereafter, time will begin and teams will be advised to *throw when ready*. Competing teams will then have 90 seconds in which to complete as many attempts as desired. Canines must not cross the

Great disc dogs make second efforts. Throwing into the wind will give your dog time to recover from a mistimed jump.

SVEN VAN DRIESSCHE (SEQUENCE)

throwing line until the disc leaves the thrower's hand or a throwing fault will be called. The thrower may not step on, or over, the line at the time of the throw or a foot fault will be called. A canine may be restrained, anywhere behind the throwing line, with the aid of a helper, if desired. Catches will be measured from the throwing line to the point where the rear-most paw of the canine contacts the ground at the time of the catch. Successfully caught tipped throws will be counted as being caught at the point where the canine first made contact with the disc regardless of the point that the canine actually became in full possession of the disc. If a disc leaves the thrower's hand before the 90-second throwing period elapses, it will be scored. Competitors may change discs between throws as long as the discs are permitted in the Class in which the competitor is competing.

Competitors may, in the Hyperflite XDC, choose to throw any safe plastic disc that was designed specifically for canine use (no golf discs) as long as the chosen disc also meets the weight requirements of the Class in which the team is competing.

Two Competitive Divisions: Men's and Women's.

Three Competitive Classes, Light (less than 85 grams), Classic (90 to 110 grams), and Unlimited (more than 110 grams).

COMPETITOR ELIGIBILITY

Local Championships Hyperflite Skyhoundz (U.S. and International) Local Championships are free events, open to all competitors regardless of experience. You are welcome to enter as many Hyperflite Skyhoundz Local Championships as you like and there are no geographic restrictions.

U.S. Regional Qualifiers Registration fees apply. Prequalification is not required. Eligibility for Hyperflite Skyhoundz U.S. Regional Qualifiers is based on residence in a geographic region as follows:

North Central Region Competitors from the following states are eligible to compete in the North Central Regional: Illinois, Indiana, Iowa, Kansas, Kentucky, Michigan, Minnesota, Missouri, Nebraska, North Dakota, Ohio, South Dakota, and Wisconsin.

Northeast Region Competitors from the following states are eligible to compete in the Northeast Regional: Connecticut, Delaware, District of Columbia, Maine, Maryland, Massachusetts, New Hampshire, New Jersey, New York, Pennsylvania, Rhode Island, Vermont, Virginia, and West Virginia.

Northwest Region Competitors from the following states are eligible to compete in the Northwest Regional: Alaska, Colorado, Idaho, Montana, Oregon, Utah, Washington, and Wyoming.

South Central Region Competitors from the following states are eligible to compete in the South Central Regional: Arkansas, Louisiana, Mississippi, New Mexico, Oklahoma, and Texas.

Southeast Region Competitors from the following states are eligible to compete in the Southeast Regional: Alabama, Florida, Georgia, North Carolina, South Carolina, and Tennessee.

Southwest Region Competitors from the following states are eligible to compete in the Southwest Regional: Arizona, California, and Nevada.

Open Qualifiers Hyperflite/Skyhoundz stages two Open Qualifiers (Eastern and Western U.S.). Anyone may compete in the Open Qualifiers and there are no geographic limitations for competitor entry.

International Qualifiers International Qualifiers for the Hyperflite Skyhoundz World Championship are held in a number of countries. Competitors from Canada are eligible to compete in any Hyperflite Skyhoundz Qualifier held in Canada. Competitors from any European Country may compete in any Hyperflite Skyhoundz Qualifier held in Europe. Competitors from Asian countries may compete in any International Qualifier held in any country in Asia. U.S. Residents are not eligible to earn invitations to the World Championship at an International Qualifier, but may compete for awards.

World Championship Invitations to the Hyperflite Skyhoundz World Championship are awarded at Hyperflite Skyhoundz Regional, Open, and International Qualifiers.

PETER BLOEME

Chuck Middleton and "Flash."

Hyperflite DiscDogathons Hyperflite DiscDogathons are open to all competitors regardless of experience. Competitors are welcome to enter as many Hyperflite DiscDogathons as they like and there are no geographic restrictions.

Hyperflite Xtreme Distance Challenge
Hyperflite Xtreme Distance Challenge events are open to all competitors regardless of experience. Competitors are welcome to enter as many Hyperflite Xtreme Distance Challenge events as they like and there are no geographic restrictions.

SKYHOUNDZ COMPETITION FORMATS
Local Championships Hyperflite Skyhoundz Local Championships are held in many cities, states, and countries. All Hyperflite Skyhoundz Local Championships consist of either:

A) Two 60-second rounds of Distance/Accuracy with winners determined by combining the scores from both rounds of Distance/Accuracy; or

B) Freestyle and Distance/Accuracy Combined: One 90-second round of Freestyle and one 60-second round of Distance/Accuracy with winners determined by doubling the Freestyle score and adding it to the Distance/Accuracy score.

Contact the local host to verify the competition format. If more than 25 teams compete, the local host may limit participation in the second round to the top 6-10 scoring teams from the first round.

Skyhoundz Regional, Open and International Qualifiers Hyperflite Regional, Open and International Qualifiers consist of the same four Championship Divisions: Open Division, Sport Division, MicroDog Division, and Pairs Freestyle Division.

Within those Championship Divisions, competitors may choose to compete in different Classes and thereby have their scores evaluated relative to several peer groups. Awards are given to the top three finishers in all Classes. Available Classes vary from Division to Division.

Important Note: Only Expert Class entries are eligible to receive invitations to the World Championship. Therefore, you must specify on your registration form that you wish to enter in the Expert Class, of the applicable Division(s), in order to compete for an invitation to the World Championship.

If a team chooses to compete in multiple Classes within a particular Division, then the competitor will only need to compete once in that Division, during the final rounds, to have the score counted for purposes of determining the team's finish in each Class within such Division.

Open Division (Freestyle and Distance/Accuracy Combined) The Open Division provides opportunities to compete in Expert, Masters, Novice, and Youth Classes. The top four Expert Class teams receive invitations to the World Championship.

Round 1 — Freestyle elimination round to the top six teams in each class

Sven Van Driessche

Praise is the best reward for a job well done.

followed by Round 2 — Distance/Accuracy and Round 3 — Freestyle. First round scores are used for elimination and then dropped. A team's final score is determined by taking the third round Freestyle score and doubling it and then adding it to the Distance/Accuracy score.

Open Division Tie-Breaker If there is a tie for first, second, third or fourth place in the Expert Class or first, second or third place in the other classes, the tie will be broken by the following criteria, as necessary: 1) The team with the highest combined scores in the Athleticism and Wow!Factor categories from the Freestyle Rounds, 2) The team with the highest score in Distance/Accuracy. 3) A Face-off round will take place with each team receiving one Distance/Accuracy throw. The dog making the higher scoring catch will be declared the victor. If the teams are still tied after each has made one throw, Face-off continues until one dog makes a higher scoring catch than

the other. Officials will permit the competitors to rest their dogs as necessary.

Sport Division (Distance/Accuracy) The Sport Division provides opportunities to compete in Expert, Masters, Novice, Youth, and Team Classes. — The top four Expert Class teams receive invitations to the World Championship.

Round 1 — Distance/Accuracy elimination round to the top six teams in each class. Round 2 — Distance/Accuracy. Final scores are cumulative.

Sport Division Tie-Breaker If there is a tie for first, second, third, or fourth place in the Expert Class or first, second or third place in the other Classes, the tie will be broken by the following criteria, as necessary: 1) The team with the fewest throws in both rounds, 2) A Face-off round with each team receiving one Distance/Accuracy throw. The dog making the higher scoring catch will be declared the victor. If the teams are still tied after each has made one throw,

Face-off continues until one dog makes a higher scoring catch than the other. Officials will permit the competitors to rest their dogs as necessary.

MicroDog Division (Freestyle and Distance/Accuracy Combined) The MicroDog Division provides opportunities to compete in Expert Class only. —The top two Expert Class teams receive invitations to the World Championship.

MicroDogs must weigh less than 25 pounds or be 16, or fewer, inches tall as measured from the ground to a point midway between the shoulders and hips as determined by Skyhoundz officials.

MicroDog competitors must use the *K-10 Pup*, (*Competition Standard Pup, FrostBite Pup, Jawz Pup, or SofFlite Pup disc*) or a similar or smaller-sized solid plastic disc made by another manufacturer.

Round 1 — Freestyle elimination to the top six teams followed by Round 2 — Distance/Accuracy and Round 3 — Freestyle. First round scores are used for elimination and then dropped. A team's final score is determined by taking the third round Freestyle score and doubling it and then adding it to the Distance/Accuracy score.

Because some MicroDog Division teams also desire to compete in the Open Division, and because the two Divisions have identical formats, competing teams only need to compete once, at Regional, Open, and International Qualifiers, to be scored in both Divisions. However, in order for scores to count in the MicroDog Division, MicroDog teams must use the smaller discs described previously in all rounds. There are no disc size limits in the Open Division.

MicroDog Tie-Breaker If there is a tie for first or second place, the tie will be broken by the following criteria, as necessary: 1) The team with the highest combined scores in the Athleticism

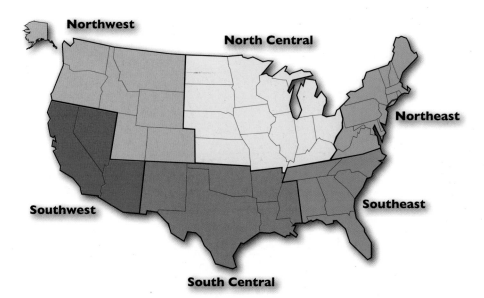

Hyperflite Skyhoundz Geographic Regions for U.S. Regional Qualifiers

and Wow!Factor categories from the Freestyle Rounds, 2) The team with the highest score in Distance/Accuracy, 3) A Face-off round will take place with each team receiving one Distance/Accuracy throw. The dog making the higher scoring catch will be declared the victor. If the teams are still tied after each has made one throw, Face-off continues until one dog makes a higher scoring catch than the other. Officials will permit the competitors to rest their dogs as necessary.

Pairs Freestyle Division (Freestyle Only) The Pairs Freestyle Division pro-vides opportunities to compete in Expert Class only. Teams compete in one Freestyle round (two Freestyle rounds at the World Championship) — The top two teams receive invitations to the World Championship.

Pairs Freestyle Tie-Breaker If there is a tie for first, or second place, the tie will be broken by the following criteria, as necessary: 1) The team with the highest combined scores in the Athleticism and Wow!Factor categories from the Freestyle Round(s), 2) A Snapshot round will take place with each team alternating

Either Danny Venegas is reversing the expected, by herding his Border Collie as part of his Freestyle preroutine or he's praying to the disc dog gods for a perfect routine.

turns and receiving ten seconds in which to demonstrate their strongest trick or cluster of tricks. Order of competition will be determined by a coin toss. The timekeeper will announce the start of Snapshot when each competitor signals his or her readiness to begin. The judges will then declare a winner based on their impressions of the overall quality of the Snapshot performances.

Recreational Division (TimeTrial) The Recreational Division provides opportunities to compete in Expert, Novice, Youth, and Team Classes but is an optional event at Regional, Open, and International Qualifiers. Teams compete in a round of TimeTrial and compete for awards only. No invitations to the World Championship are extended in this Division.

Recreational Division Tie-Breaker If there is a tie for first, second or third place, the tie will be broken by additional TimeTrial rounds between the tied teams until one team achieves a faster time. Officials will permit the competitors to rest their dogs as necessary.

Sven Van Driessche

Judges love to see interesting throws — like this "air bounce" — in competition.

On a hot day, a dip in the pond feels great.

Sven Van Driessche (Sequence)

SKYHOUNDZ COMPETITION CLASS DESCRIPTIONS

Competitive Classes, vary from Division to Division, and apply only to Hyperflite Skyhoundz Regional, Open, and International Qualifiers.

Expert Anyone can enter.

Masters Dogs 9 years and older (as of the date of the competition entered). A canine registered in the Masters Class may not simultaneously be entered in the Expert Class.

Novice A team composed of a canine and thrower that, either together or separately, have never finished higher than fourth place at any Hyperflite Skyhoundz Regional, Open Qualifier or International Qualifier in any of the following Divisions: Open Division, Sport Division, MicroDog Division, or Pairs Freestyle Division.

Youth Youngsters 14 years and younger (as of the date of the competition entered).

Team Teams must be **male/female** unless one of the team members is under 16 years of age in which case the team members can be of the same sex. In team class, throwers alternate throws.

COMPETITION SCHEDULES

LINK For a schedule of Local Championship Events and Hyperflite DiscDogathons please visit: http://skyhoundz.com/localschedule.html

LINK For a schedule of Regional Qualifiers and Open Qualifiers, please visit: http://skyhoundz.com/usregional-championships.html

LINK For a schedule of International Qualifiers, please visit: http://skyhoundz.com/internationalchampionships.html

LINK For information on the World Championship, please visit: http://skyhoundz.com/worldchampionship.html

FORMATS AND JUDGING

Whether you compete in a Hyperflite-sponsored disc dog event, or an event sponsored or staged by another organizer, a thorough understanding of the contest rules will give you the best chance of success on the playing field. Many competitors choose to *do it their own way* and compete in the manner in which they are accustomed to competing. This approach is fine, but if you don't adapt your style to the rules and regulations of the other series, then don't expect to enjoy the same level of success that you have experienced in the past. It can be quite a shock to practice a freestyle routine for months using seven discs, only to arrive at an event and learn that only five discs are permitted in competition. There are numerous subtle differences between

Watch me catch this disc while balancing on one paw.

Jay Moldow

Competitor meetings are an excellent time to make sure you are familiar with all the rules of the event.

the various series. Rather than lamenting the *headache* caused by having to shift competitive gears, revel in the differences and distinctions between the events. Use your knowledge of the rules to gain advantage over your fellow competitors. Most contest series have competitor briefings immediately before the competition begins. Attend these briefings and pay attention. If you have a question, even one you think is silly, ask it anyway. Judges love to hear themselves talk!

In the end, you can do everything right and still not receive the scores that you expect. There is frequently a big difference between the experience level of the judges at a local contest judged by park and recreation staff and a regional level event judged by experienced disc dog judges. We were once told by a World Champion, that, in the year he won the Worlds, he also finished 11th at a local competition. Keep things in perspective, and remember to have fun!

If you are an experienced competitor, think of Local Championships as *spring training* for the regular season Regional and DiscDogathon events judged by more experienced officials.

PRACTICE STRATEGY

A common problem that we see in competition is the reluctance of some Freestyle competitors to practice Distance/Accuracy events. These competitors often don't succeed in competition, not because they aren't skilled, but because they choose not to work as hard at distance events as they do with Freestyle. If a team can lose a competition based upon Distance/Accuracy scores, then they can just as easily win the competition based upon those scores. Our view is that an Open Division World Champion should be proficient in both disciplines. Historically, World Champions have always been required to demonstrate Distance/Accuracy proficiency. So, why not work hard at the discipline and use it as a way to re-

gain lost ground, after a less-than-perfect Freestyle round, or to distinguish yourself from the competition when everyone is nailing Freestyle.

FREESTYLE PRE-ROUTINES

At most disc dog competitions, time begins as soon as a disc is released, thrown, or moved from a set position. A pre-routine, therefore, is everything that happens on the playing field leading up to the first throw. Pre-routines are not timed or scored. So, why do they matter, you might ask?

While pre-routines are not scored, they can be very beneficial in that they set the tone for the routine to come. They also help focus the attention of the crowd on you and your canine. They present an opportunity for you to put smiles on the faces of the judges. A happy judge might just give you the benefit of the doubt on a close call.

Pre-routines should be short affairs that don't make you look like an idiot, unless the *idiot theme* is part of your overall master plan for world domination! Sometimes a pre-routine is nothing more than the manner in which you and your canine arrive on the field of play prior to competing. On a hot day, a long pre-routine can cause your dog to become overheated before he even makes his first catch. Be warned that elaborate pre-routines can also focus attention on an early failure. Many times, as judges, we have watched painfully-long pre-routines that culminate in an ugly miss. If poorly executed, a pre-routine can hurt your relationship with the crowd. Cheering crowds can motivate you and *Rover* to play beyond your abilities and seize the day.

Finally, be sure to practice your pre-routine. Consult your spouse or significant other who will probably offer an honest assessment of your *dance*

Sven Van Driessche (Sequence)

A short pre-routine which flows into Freestyle can help set the tone for your routine.

moves before you humiliate yourself in front of a group of total strangers! And please, unless you have washboard abs, consider eliminating the belly-dancing sequence from your pre-routine...especially before breakfast!

FREESTYLE CHOREOGRAPHY AND MUSICAL SELECTION

When we began to compete, at the turn of the century (it feels that way sometimes), nearly all of the top teams performed to music. But, very few teams actually choreographed their routines to the music. Rehearsed choreography (this doesn't have to be elaborate) is now fairly standard for elite-level competitors. Although choreography does not have to precisely sync with the music, the pace and flow of your routine should fit the music that you select. High points in your music should coincide with high points in your routine. When you practice freestyle, take a portable music player with you and practice to your chosen music. Working out to the same song every time will make it easier to remember the correct sequence of moves so you don't leave something out. Break your routine into three or four segments (sometimes referred to as *memory groupings*) and practice segments independently as well as in sequence. It is easier to remember four groups of five tricks, than 20 consecutive tricks. On competition day, don't forget to bring your musical recording with you to the competition! Better yet, bring two copies, just in case. In our day competitors brought their music on 78 rpm records or 8-track tapes, but you will want to bring a CD of your favorite selection. If possible, burn a CD with just your chosen musical selection. That way, the sound system operator won't accidentally select the wrong track and force you to spend more time than necessary in the hot summer sun waiting for your music to be properly cued. Mark your CD with your dog's name so you can retrieve it later.

Although judges do not score music, a good song selection can arguably impact your scores for other reasons. For example, let's assume that there are two competitors with identical dogs and routines. The first competes with no music. The crowd watches politely and claps on occasion. Some in the audience pay

A "costume" yes, but embarrassing none-the-less.

Peter Bloeme

Jeff Hoot

Beer, no matter what the brand, is not an appropriate adult pre-routine for competition.

Their interest is piqued and they want the team to do well and live up to the energy and excitement of the music. The crowd's energy and excitement is passed along to the competitor and to the competitor's dog. This gets the team more involved in their routine and they push a little harder and perform a little better. Since their performance is better, the judges award them higher scores. It doesn't matter what your music is though it is always a good idea to select music with a broad appeal that suits your personality and the tempo of your routine. In all cases, music should be suitable for a family audience. Don't shock your sponsor and the parents of the wee ones in attendance with an uncensored intrusion into their afternoon of fun.

APPEARANCE/COSTUMES

attention, others talk with their friends or look elsewhere. The next competitor begins with a popular, crowd-pleasing and upbeat tune. The crowd perks up and takes a greater interest in the action. The mood of the crowd improves.

If you want to be scored like a pro then it is always a good idea to dress for the part. Although there is no scoring category for appearance, don't ignore the psychological effect that your appearance can have on the judges. You are participating in an athletic endeavor.

Sven Van Driessche

There's nothing like a happy judge!

If you wander onto the field wearing ratty-looking jeans or street shoes, it's conceivable that the competition judges won't take you seriously. A smartly-dressed athlete, in any sport, can exude confidence that can encourage an enthusiastic crowd response and a positive reception from the judges. As indicated previously, competitors who are able to get the crowd behind them often turn in performances that far exceed what they could accomplish without this emotional boost. Be sure to follow the rules of the contest organizer in so far as costumes for human and canine are concerned.

FREESTYLE INNOVATION AND CREATIVITY

There are obvious ways to improve your scores, like practicing Distance/Accuracy in all wind and weather conditions, and indirect ways, such as through musical selection and appearance. In Freestyle, innovation is the most significant score multiplier. If you show the judges well-executed tricks and moves that they haven't seen before, you'll likely score well. To really be an innovative performer you must trend toward the obsessive in the way that you approach Freestyle. By that we mean you have to be willing to try different things even if they are outside of your comfort zone. One particularly innovative competitor once confessed to leaving a pad and pencil by his bed in case he had an inspiration in his dreams. Upon awakening, he would write the trick down and later try it with his dog. Try anything and everything that you can imagine and use whatever works in your routine. While you are trying new things, have someone video your practice sessions. In reviewing the video, you may find that some moves you thought looked

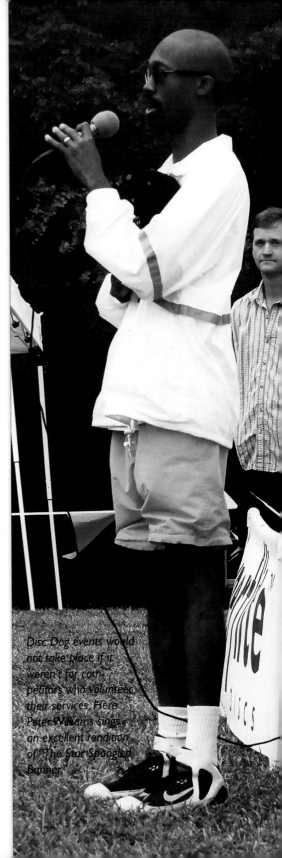

Disc Dog events would not take place if it weren't for competitors who volunteer their services. Here Peter Williams sings an excellent rendition of "The Star Spangled Banner."

Sven Van Driessche

Sven Van Driessche

As far as costumes go, regardless of heritage, some people naturally look better in skirts than others.

great were not nearly as impressive as pictured in your mind's eye. The reverse can also be true.

Regardless of how perfectly you execute the tricks in your routine, they will soon seem average when compared to the routines of other top competitors who are constantly pushing the limits, searching for tricks that have never before been accomplished. Innovation helps to explain how dog/owner teams like Gary Suzuki and Soarin' *Sam*, Chris Breit and *Mattie*, or Danny Eggleston and *Guinan* can appear seemingly out of nowhere and finish in the top one, two or three spots at the World Championship.

Sometimes, innovation is as simple as putting a new variation on a familiar move. Better yet are unique new tricks that *drop the jaws* of spectators and judges alike. You know the ones we mean. The tricks that make you turn to

the person standing next to you and say...*did you see that?*

Innovation requires brainstorming. Bring seemingly disparate disciplines into your routine if possible. Many innovative disc tricks utilize elements of ballet or dance. Other tricks have their origin in sports such as soccer, gymnastics or croquet (well, maybe not croquet). Still other tricks will be the result of a compromise between a trick that you imagine and the realities of the physical limitations of you and your canine. For example, the inventor of the behind the back canine catch confessed that the trick was actually a compromise trick that evolved from an attempted 360° spinning catch. Since the competitor could only make it half way around, he thought, *I wonder if I can catch my dog behind my back?* Voila! Do not give up on a good idea merely be-

Peter Williams demonstrates the "Spin Cycle," a move in which the canine is spun around the thrower's body and gently returned to the ground.

Sven Van Driessche (Sequence)

Judges always need to be on their toes. Here, even though the catch was made Mark Jennings, makes the OB call.

cause you experience limited success at first. Sometimes all that is needed is a slight modification to solve what seems to be an unsolvable problem. Be patient as you experiment with new and innovative tricks, and remember, if you can imagine it, with a little practice you can probably accomplish it. With hard work, you can perfect it.

FREESTYLE DISC MANAGEMENT

Proper disc management requires you to confirm that you have the proper quantity of discs in hand before you walk onto the playing field. At nearly every event we have ever judged, at least one competitor will take the field with one-too-many discs. Of course, there is a lot more to disc management than counting discs. Making optimal use of the time that you are allocated requires that you master the concept of disc management and incorporate good disc management principles into your routine. When you plan your routine, it must not only flow well and look good, but your discs must remain close at hand or you will waste

Sven Van Driessche (Sequence)

"Butterfly" throw sequence to a MicroDog.

time retrieving them. The best disc doggers plan their routines so that, within seconds, they can gather up the discs dropped by their canines and be ready to launch into the next sequence.

There are many ways to approach the disc management dilemma. The *Rule of Thirds* is one such way. It holds that the field is divided into thirds, and wherever the canine may venture, the thrower should never leave the middle third of the field. Indeed, smart disc doggers usually do stay at home in the middle third

of the playing field while letting their canines venture into the outer thirds of the field. This makes good sense when you consider that the judges in freestyle competitions generally congregate at the proverbial 50-yard line, where most of the action is located. If you want to be certain that your *best stuff* is seen by those who put the magic numbers on your score sheet, then you will definitely want to stay close to field center. Additionally, when your canine jumps in close proximity to the judges, the jumps will often appear to

them to be higher than they would if the jumps occurred at a distance. That's not to say that you shouldn't be moving and making use of the field, but don't venture far from home. Naturally, you will want to send your canine into the outer reaches of the field, to demonstrate quickness and speed, but you sure don't want to scatter your discs all over creation and then waste your valuable time chasing after them.

Competitors who leave the comfort zone at field center often experience two bad things. First, they may find that they have moved so far from the judges that the nuances of their routines are no longer observable. Second, if they have managed to maneuver to the upwind end of the field, then all throws back toward the middle third will be downwind and difficult for the canine to catch up to. Don't let your canine dictate where you end up on the field. Reposition your canine as necessary to stay in the middle third of the field.

It is also a good idea to cluster all of your multiple series and close-in work early in your routine. Use occasional long throws to your canine to buy time to retrieve dropped discs. By the time your dog returns with disc in mouth, you should have all of your discs in hand and be ready to go with your next series of tricks. If you want to incorporate really long throws into your routine — a potentially risky thing to do — then go long at the end of your routine when disc retrieval is no longer an issue.

To improve your disc management skills head to the park on canine rest days and practice your freestyle routine — sans canine. As you work through your sequences, make the throws exactly as you would if you were competing. Then, smoothly and quickly gather up the discs and proceed to the point on the playing field that will be the launching point for each successive sequence. Since many tricks are wind sensitive, you should work the field just as you would if you were actually competing with your dog. Don't try and look cool and do the *Hol-*

lywood jog because you will only waste valuable time. Instead, move quickly and deliberately as you gather your discs.

If you want to see good disc management in action then, unfortunately, competition videos will probably be a disappointment. Since the canine is always the focus of the cameraman, very little disc management behavior will be observable. It's always best to journey to a regional level competition or even the World Championship and watch the top teams in action. Instead of watching the canines, focus on the trainer and watch how he or she moves to retrieve discs and position the canine so as to keep the action close at hand. The seemingly effortless manner in which elite level teams maneuver on the playing field is no accident. If you want to win competitions, then you will need to become an expert at disc management.

WIND

Never has a word struck more terror in the hearts of disc doggers than the word **wind**! We eagerly watch weather reports and consult higher authorities, when necessary, all to minimize the impact of *Mariah* on our performances. But wind isn't really mysterious at all. In fact, it can be your best friend. Remember the saying, *the enemy of my enemy is my friend*. Since fear of the wind is so universal among competitors, why not make the wind your friend and gain an ally in your competitive endeavors. Wouldn't it be nice if strong winds actually gave you a competitive advantage? Once you understand the wind, then you can work with it and even use it to gain an edge over your fellow competitors.

For any performance or competition, it is helpful to think of the wind in micro-meteorological terms. Wind doesn't just blow. It moves over, around and through things accelerating, rising, and falling, in ways that are more predictable than you might think. If you have

Even dogs have egos...

ever seen currents in a river make small eddies and ripples, then you can imagine that air behaves in a similar way when it moves around or over objects.

Turbulence may result from the passage of the wind over nearby structures or trees. Occasionally those structures may provide an exploitable break from the wind just as a boulder in a river might make a calm eddy for a smart fish. Or, the wind may create strong down drafts and dead areas that will make you want to cry out for your mother. Be aware of your surroundings. Use your knowledge of the micro-meterological impact that trees, buildings and terrain have on the wind to your advantage. It is pretty well established that top competitors endeavor to wind-proof their routines. But anyone can stack the odds in their favor by carefully observing the impact of the wind on the competitors who take the field first. These *wind dummies* (a name that is affectionately given to hang glider pilots who are the first to fly on a particularly rowdy day) can show you the path to follow when it's

your turn to take the field. But you have to be observant and apply what you have learned.

Avoid following the pack, especially if *the pack* is being trounced by the wind gods. Instead, make your own way. You may be able to concentrate your activities in an area of the competition field that is shielded from the wind by nearby structures. Or perhaps an open section of the field will prove to be better because it might not be as affected by the turbulence associated with the movement of wind over trees or objects. Since we can't see the wind, we have to visualize its movement by observing the effect it has on the discs we throw. Prior to competing, get out on the field and throw from each part of the field in various directions. This should help you establish the best location in which to perform as well as tell you what adjustments to make to ensure maximum success. On those ultra-windy days, forget about staying close to field center and move wherever you must to minimize the impact of the wind.

At one of the windiest World Championships ever, during the Distance/Accuracy round, only one competitor chose to throw into the wind. On that day, the wind was so strong that this competitor was practically scraping the outside edge of the disc on the ground because of the copious amount of *hyzer* required to keep his discs from turning over in the gale. Not coincidentally, he received the highest score in the Distance/Accuracy round for his efforts. If you can't make good throws into the wind with lots of *hyzer*, that doesn't mean that you should choose not to throw into the wind. It means you should learn to throw with more *hyzer!* You might also elect to use a heavier disc like the *Jawz* or *Jawz X-Comp*. You would never want to throw a heavier disc, like the *Jawz*, downwind. But throwing into the wind means that even heavier discs will float longer, and

your dog will have plenty of time to catch up to the disc, throttle down, and make a great catch.

If the wind is a crosswind, be sure to adjust your delivery so that your throws do not carry off of the field of play. It shouldn't take more than one bad throw to convince you of the need to make adjustments. Your ultimate goal should be consistent, predictable results in any conditions that may occur.

It goes without saying that practice makes perfect. But make sure that you practice in *all* wind and weather conditions. Deliberately choose those awful windy and rainy days and do your best to make the best out of the conditions present. Competitions can be won by the best prepared teams as easily as they can be won by the most athletic teams.

Finally, know when to leave a difficult trick out of your routine. If the wind is gusting to thirty miles per hour and the discs are wet with rain, you may want to

From small to tall, all dogs love to catch flying discs.

Peter Bloeme

Peter Bloeme

skip your *spinning triple wifferdill with the half-monty delivery*.

Make the wind your friend and you will have the confidence it takes to excel when others falter.

COMPETITION STRATEGY

Our best advice is to have one! You should know the relevant competition rules long before you arrive at the competition. Don't overwork your canine in the minutes before you compete. It pains us to think of the countless world-class routines that have been *left on the sidelines* by trainers who, in the moments before competing, exhausted their canines by needlessly practicing their routines out of nervousness.

As you and your canine step onto the playing field, take a few seconds to relax. With due consideration given to the wind, position yourself and your canine in the ideal spot to commence your routine. As you begin, remember that you are master and commander on the playing field. Never cede creative control to your canine. If you feel that you are losing control, pause, reposition your dog and continue. Your success will be a byproduct of your attitude. Your canine needs to know that you believe in him and if he senses that from you, then he won't let you down.

WORKING WITH THE MEDIA AT COMPETITIONS

Since canine disc sports tend to draw the attention of the media, there are some basic rules to keep in mind that will guide you in your interactions with members of *the fourth estate* during both competitions and exhibitions.

Canine disc competitions are the most fun you and your canine will likely experience together. But, without the sponsorship of flying disc companies

An example of a "juggling" sequence.

Sven Van Driessche (Sequence)

Sven Van Driessche (Sequence)

and other pet-centric entities, the competition scene would not be nearly as vibrant. Sponsors receive, as the primary benefit of their sponsorship, media impressions from the print and television press that cover the sponsored event. Therefore, do your best to accommodate any reasonable media requests, as long as they don't interfere with your competition preparations. Maintain a professional demeanor and be supportive of the sponsor in the quantity and quality of your comments.

When you are competing, you do not have to let a cameraperson (still or video) control your actions. You and the media will sometimes have opposing agendas. You want your canine to make a great catch while photographers and videographers want to be right there to film it when it happens. As you and your canine gain experience, you will grow comfortable working in proximity to these media professionals. You will be able to demonstrate your best stuff only a few feet from the lens. But, when you are *media green,* these folks can be intimidating. Don't let the media spoil your day. If you are nervous about the location of a cameraperson or photographer, let the judges know before you start competing and they will politely ask the media representative to move.

Video cameras are expensive and in our years of working with the media, we have had several incidents where cameras costing as much as European sports cars have been totalled. Dogs are, apparently, of stouter disposition than the video cameras used by TV stations. On the bright side, the video obtained is usually spectacular and always a highlight on canine disc blooper films. Nevertheless, woe falls heavy on the

Sven Van Driessche (Sequence)

For the best disc management try to pick up discs while the audience's attention is focused on your dog.

cameraman that damages one and he or she will appreciate being warned of imminent danger.

News crews, reporters, or the event sponsor may sometimes ask you to perform on camera before, or between rounds of a competition. Since doing so can tire your dog and seriously affect your performance, you are welcome to politely inform the reporter or sponsor that you will be happy to spend some time on camera after the contest concludes. If you choose to perform for the media, don't wear your dog out. Just a few quick moves and then rest and water your canine. Don't worry about grabbing all the *face time* you can because, over the course of your canine disc career, you will likely have many opportunities to appear on camera. Most disc doggers do.

When working with a camera crew, ask them what they are looking for and help them find a good position in which to shoot the desired images or video. Give them a brief demo of the types of tricks that your canine can do so they can begin to think about how they want to film or shoot the action. For still photography, the venerable *backflip* often produces spectacular images. Video can capture the fluidity and complexity of a trick sequence and you can pull out all the stops when the tape is rolling. Finally, it should go without saying that your first responsibility is for your dog's safety. Do not let a camera person persuade you to do something that you don't feel is safe for your canine. You should refuse to work on asphalt, concrete or in extreme heat. Also, if you make a studio appearance, on the grounds of a televi-

When working with the media, keep your dog's safety in mind.

sion station, do not let your canine off leash or throw to him if he might inadvertently end up on a busy roadway. Rest your dog as needed and keep him properly hydrated.

Anytime you work with the media, always represent our sport as professionally and enthusiastically as you can. Be prompt, courteous and accommodating. Answer questions from reporters or news anchors in brief sound bites and — if you have time — try and mention the sponsor's name at some point in your interview. Sponsors always appreciate any plugs you can give them. Look at the interviewer, rather than the camera, when answering questions on camera and speak clearly. Finally, it is acceptable to ask if you can have a copy of the photos or video shot at an interview, although this may not always be possible. You will find that being a professional with the media, in addition to keeping the sponsor happy, will also earn you the respect and admiration of your peers.

Sven-Van Driessche

And they say his bark is worse than his bite!

You're a disc dogger now and you'll soon be travelling with the pack to disc dog competitions. Perhaps you will drive to a nearby Hyperflite Skyhoundz Local Championship, or maybe you will even journey by air to the World Championship or some other exotic destination.

Regardless of the mode of travel you select, you will want to acquire an airline-approved kennel (sometimes referred to as a crate) to serve as a traveling dog house for your canine companion. Kennels can be purchased at most pet stores as well as online at web retailers. Be sure to buy the kennel in time to acclimate your canine to it before you begin your travels. Clearly and permanently mark your kennel with identifying information including your dog's name and your cell phone number. Do this on the top and sides of the kennel with a black Sharpie marker. The kennel should have a piece of carpet or other absorbent material on the floor along with water and food cups. These are required for airline travel.

Jeff Perry and "Gilbert" waiting patiently at the airport.

Peter Bloeme

Peter Bloeme

If your dogs are flying with you, it's always a good idea to keep an eye out for them.

It is very important to purchase the correct-sized kennel. Your canine should be able to stand up and turn around easily without banging his head on the kennel ceiling. The kennel you purchase should also be approved for air travel and have manufactured openings that provide ventilation on the kennel sides and ends. Also, make sure the locking mechanism on the kennel is designed with redundant systems to prevent your dog from escaping at the most inopportune moments. Trust us, great escapes have happened before…to our own dogs no less.

Once your dog is generally comfortable spending time in his transportable home, you can simulate the effect of flying by taking your dog for a ride in the car while he is safely ensconced in his kennel. When traveling, don't overload your dog's kennel with a lot of junk. Do provide bedding appropriate to the season and a favorite chew-proof toy. Don't leave discs in the kennel because

you never want to encourage your dog to chew on canine discs. Discs are for catching, not chewing! Also, don't feed your dog immediately before driving or flying as they may answer nature's call inside their kennels. The last thing you want to see when you arrive at your destination is the inside of your brand-new kennel painted with the contents of your canine's most recent meal.

AIR TRAVEL

Once, while traveling with our world champion canines, we had the unique pleasure of departing from gate K-9. That was a welcomed omen. Over the course of our long involvement in canine disc sports we have travelled with our dogs via nearly every form of transportation possible, including high-speed bullet trains in Japan, limousines in the Big Apple, pedi-cabs in Atlantic City, water taxis in Florida and even a chartered double-decker bus in Spain. Of all the ways that you can travel from point A to Point B, air travel is often the most

Peter Bloeme (Sequence)

"Wizard's" Great Adventure: "Wizard's" kennel getting tagged, taken off the truck, loaded onto a belt, approaching the underbelly of a plane, in the plane with baggage, and arriving at baggage claim.

frightening and frustrating for you and your canine teammate. Although some airlines will allow celebrity pets to travel in the cabin of the aircraft – most don't.

Do notify the airline that you will be traveling with a pet because you'll usually need to make a special reservation for him. The pet transportation fee is considerably less than a coach class ticket. Your dog's travel voucher cannot be purchased through your travel agent. However, once you have your own ticket in hand, you can buy your dog's travel voucher in advance at the airport or at an airline ticket office. Buy a round-trip transportation voucher for your dog to prevent delays on your return leg. Most states require that you have in your possession, when you travel by air, certain pet health documentation and vaccination records. Your veterinarian can examine your pet and provide the appropriate forms to you.

For trips departing from, or connecting through, areas that experience extreme temperatures, most airlines have special rules and requirements. Some airlines even have seasonal embargoes

GRAVY

Yukihiro Sekiguchi is a kind man. He loves children and dogs. Sekiguchi is enthusiastic, soft-spoken and warm-hearted. He is also as modest in victory as he is gracious in defeat. Years ago, Sekiguchi was one of the first international competitors to compete in the Skyhoundz Championship in the U.S. In short, Sekiguchi represents well the finest traditions of canine disc sports. So, it was completely in character for him to willingly volunteer his time, when asked, to do a disc dog demonstration for a group of 20 autistic children at a special children's school in Japan.

When the appointed day arrived, Sekiguchi, or "Sekiguchi-san" as we sometimes call him, journeyed to the school to give the kids a show they would never forget. At the conclusion of the action, Sekiguchi asked the kids if they would like to throw to his dog. Beaming faces told him the answer to that question.

"OK," Sekiguchi commanded in a loud voice, "Line up and you can each make a throw to my dog." What Sekiguchi didn't know, was that autistic children don't respond especially well to loud voices and, similarly, they are not great at organizing themselves into a line. Nevertheless, to the amazement of the teachers, the kids quickly complied and happily took turns tossing to Sekiguchi's eager canine. When Sekiguchi relates this story to others — years later — it is always with awe that the life-altering power of the disc dog experience can so profoundly impact the lives of those who participate in it.

*Peter Bloeme, Jeff Perry, and Alex Stein helped
bring down the Berlin Wall in Germany.*

Peter Bloeme

It's not often that you see a life-size billboard containing a disc dog, but in Shanghai, China the public was treated to the sight of Jeff Perry and "K.D." looking down upon them.

that will prevent you from transporting your canine during the hot summer months. Check with your airline before you book your flight. In any case, it is always smart to travel early in the day, when temperatures are cooler for your pet. When you fly, take comfort in the knowledge that your dog will fly in a pressurized, heated and cooled compartment. Temperatures and pressures will be exactly as they are in the passenger cabin. Unfortunately, no meals or drinks are served and no frequent flyer points are awarded. When you finally arrive at your destination, you will feel anxious and nervous about your pet's status. Don't worry, it's normal to feel this way. After more than 20 years of flying, we still nervously await the arrival of our pets. But, rather than wait passively for your pet to appear, there are things you can do to *self sooth*. First, ask airline staff where traveling pets arrive. If the person you ask isn't certain,

then ask someone else until you have confidence in the answer that you are given. No two airports are alike. Pets may be delivered at the over-sized baggage claim area, or in the most unlikely looking places. Many times, you will hear your canine barking long before he is actually brought to you. Try not to have an *episode* if your pet doesn't make it to baggage claim as quickly as you would like. We have waited as long as 45 minutes for our canines. It is, of course, a good idea to let airline personnel know you are expecting a dog and to be politely persistent if minute 30 rolls past with no sign of your buddy.

If for some reason you can't travel on the same flight as your dog, he can be shipped as air cargo or air freight. In such cases, your dog's kennel is not considered excess baggage but rather, freight, so you will be charged by the weight of the kennel and canine. You will need to go to the cargo/freight terminal of the specific airline on which your dog will be flying. This freight terminal is usually found in more remote areas at airports. Make sure you check the flight times before you get to the airport so you can let them know when you want your dog to travel. Plan to arrive at least two hours before the flight. That will give the airline time to put your dog on the correct flight. Make sure that you have made arrangements for someone to retrieve your dog at the destination airport. Animal shipments are fairly common and the airlines are good about keeping dogs in cool or heated rooms as appropriate. We should all thank the various humane organizations and animal welfare groups for the excellent treatment that our pets generally experience when traveling by air.

Air travel in the U.S. is fairly straight forward compared with travel overseas. Some island countries, require that you quarantine your dog for long periods. Hawaii, for example, has a four-month quarantine. Our travels to Japan required a two-week quarantine at Narita airport. Different forms, vaccinations and veterinary inspections may be required for international travel. Check with the airline first to find out what is required to satisfy the authorities at your destination country. Have your papers in order and a contact in the destination country that can help smooth things over if problems should arise.

FOOD AND WATER

When on the road, make sure you take along an adequate supply of your pet's normal dog food. Even if his favorite food is widely available at your destination, it is generally a headache to go *dog food shopping* after a long trip. We always bring enough food for an entire trip because it is often difficult to find your pet's favorite food in a strange land. Some disc doggers take along wa-

Peter Bloeme

Travel does have its risks, for human and canine alike. Here you see "Gilbert's" partially crushed kennel. We're still wondering what could have caused this type of damage.

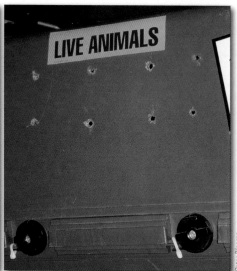

Peter Bloeme

Travel rules change all the time. One time we showed up at the airport and were told we needed holes in the back of our dogs' kennels. It wasn't easy, but we managed to make the holes with a borrowed hammer and screwdriver.

ter from home for fear that their canines may experience difficulty with the local water. However, we have never had difficulty with local water, even *en la ciudad de Mexico*. Dog's have more robust digestive systems than we do and aren't generally affected by minor variations in water quality.

HOTELS

In the early days of disc dogging it was often a challenge to find hotels that accepted canines. Now, the hospitality industry has recognized that modern American families are nearly as likely to have dogs as they are kids. Many hotel chains now happily welcome well-behaved pets. For

Serving as ambassadors and "ambassadogs" for canine disc sports is always exciting. Pictured here are Jeff Stanaway, Jeff Perry, Peter Bloeme, and Frank Montgomery sightseeing in Shanghai, China while their dogs are ordering room service.

Jeremy Angel

"Magic" soaring off Peter Bloeme's back in Japan.

travel with *all* of their family members. In Japan, Korea and China, pet owners are not so fortunate.

Being permitted to have your pet stay with you in a hotel does not give you carte blanche to let *Cujo* run amuck and frighten the other guests. You most decidedly should not let your beast mess up your hotel room or keep other guests awake with his incessant barking. As a responsible pet owner, you have an obligation to train your dog to be obedient and well behaved before you even think about taking your show on the road, so to speak. After checking in, immediately put the *do not disturb* sign on your door to prevent hotel staff from entering what has now become your dog's domain. Also, survey your room and remove, from your dog's reach, any complimentary food or candy (remember that chocolate is poisonous to dogs) that has been left in your room. Also, if you are traveling with a Border Collie or Poodle… be sure to hide the key to the minibar!

example, Starwood, La Quinta, Days Inn, Marriott, Holiday Inn, and Howard Johnsons hotels accept pets at many, if not all, of their company-owned hotels. The Motel 6, Ramada and Red Roof chains typically allow canines as well. For your protection, when booking a room with a large hotel chain, through a central reservation number, ask the operator to confirm with the destination hotel that they will accept pets.

The fact that so many hotels in the U.S. and Europe allow canines is a tremendous boon to those who want to

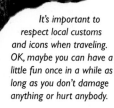

It's important to respect local customs and icons when traveling. OK, maybe you can have a little fun once in a while as long as you don't damage anything or hurt anybody.

Peter Bloeme

The safest way to perform a "vault" is low to the ground.

Collecting
Chapter 12

A surprising number of competitors collect flying discs to one degree or another. Quite a few of them have 50 to 100 discs (some have many more) hanging on their walls, packed in boxes and strewn all over. We must confess to being avid collectors ourselves and Hyperflite's warehouse has a quiet corner stuffed with thousands of older discs that trace our history in the sport and beyond.

We became collectors as most folks do, quite unintentionally. We know that collectors of all things share the same dream — that is, to accidentally stumble across an amazing trove of whatever it is they collect. We remain optimistic that, one day, we will come across an unknown cache of Frisbie's Pie Tins piled in a dark corner of a horse barn in Pennsylvania or perhaps in the storage room of a defunct bakery on Long Island. When we do, we will happily disperse these throughout the disc dog community at our cost…or will we… muwhahahahaha!

Why would a seemingly normal person, of reasonable intelligence, choose to collect discs? Because discs can be colorful, interesting, unique, historic and decorative when displayed on a wall. More importantly, they represent experiences and memories of our participation in canine disc competitions and fun times in our lives. Unfortunately, from a

canine disc collector's standpoint, there were some years in which no year was imprinted on the discs used in competition. Collecting is fun, and whether you like it or not, if you're a disc dogger you will be a disc collector as well.

Mark Wood displaying "Zach's" collection of used discs as a Halloween costume.

Peter Bloeme's story of collecting...

I actually became a collector unintentionally. I would get a tournament model here and there, or I would pick one up because it had a pretty logo. I started hanging them up neatly on the wall. Without knowing it, I had become an accumulator, or rather, a collector. Before I realized it, I owned more than 50 discs. Then, I went wild and bought, traded and acquired anything that was flat, round and could fly.

At that point, I ran out of wall space, so I designed and built special shelves to hold my favorite discs vertically—like record albums. This way, I could display more discs per foot of wall space. I put the rest into storage. As with all collectors, I eventually reached a saturation point where I had to choose a specialty (limiting myself to one color, model, size, type, etc.) I chose to concentrate on antiques, Wham-O Professional Models and the unusual. Some of my unusual discs are made out of cloth, some make sounds when thrown, some light up (not just glow), and some have strings attached so they return to the thrower. My collection now numbers in the thousands.

As a collector, I've often dreamed about walking into an old toy store and, while digging around in the back, finding some antique discs hidden away in an old, dirty, dusty box. For me, this dream actually came true. However, it wasn't an old toy store but surprisingly a new gas station.

While driving all night on a demonstration tour, I pulled into a brightly lit, new Shell gas station at 2 o'clock in the morning. I pumped my gas and went inside to pay. As I walked grogily to the counter, I realized there was something unusual about the colored plastic hubcaps, I had observed out of the corner of my eye, on top of the cigarette machine. Upon closer inspection, I discovered they were Unique U1s, antique discs I had never seen or heard of. Despite my excitement, I managed to casually ask the man at the counter where on earth he had found those old discs. He told me they had been sitting around his old gas station for years and he had just moved them to the new station to get rid of them! After negotiating a discount for "taking them all off his hands," I bought them for a song.

Some flying discs from Peter Bloeme's collection.

Katherine Ferger and "Tallulah," 2007 MicroDog World Champions.

Star Performers
Chapter 13

PERFORMING WITH YOUR CANINE

One of the neatest things we disc dog-gers get to experience is the thrill of performing in front of large crowds. Whether at an NFL halftime show, Major League Baseball game or even a county fair, it is always exhilarating to hear the roar of a crowd when you re-ally nail your routine. The experience can be quite intoxicating. However, there is a considerable amount of effort and drudgery that falls in between the hard work and those fleeting episodes of glory. When you finally do experi-ence your *ten seconds of fame* you will most definitely have memories that will last a lifetime. Not many people get the chance to stand in the middle of the field, in a packed football stadium, with

Peter Bloeme and "Wizard" on "David Letterman."

Willard Scott hamming it up with Jeff Perry and "Gilbert."

only a dog for company. And field goal kickers think that they have pressure!

Although we have always counseled disc dog enthusiasts not to quit their day jobs in order to pursue a life on the road performing canine disc shows, enough people have made a go of it to warrant some discussion of this type of lifestyle.

Over the years, disc doggers have had some interesting gigs. Some of the most interesting include the circus, animal theme parks, county fairs, Las Vegas resorts, professional sporting events and even *The Super Bowl*!

Whether you are doing shows for fun, as a sideline, or as a full-time occupation there is one constant — you should never do anything that is not in the best interest of your canine. While your dog will love the extra playing time that a week-long county fair might bring, due consideration must always be given to your canine's well being. Common

problems encountered by performers include inadequate playing surfaces, temperature extremes, not enough rest time between shows, obstacles in the performing area, and demanding organizers. The cardinal rule should always be *paws before paycheck*. Never let money cause you to ignore important safety considerations and the well-being of your best friend.

SAFETY CONSIDERATIONS

Let's say you and your trusty disc hound *Bauser* get offered a sweet gig on the famous cruise ship HMS Norwalk. Visions of babes, booze, and buffets flash through your mind! Well, before you go overboard with joy, you have a few things to think about. Number one, there's no grass. Number two, it's a long way to the water if you make a bad throw. With every gig there are many questions that must be answered.

The Crown Prince and Princess of Japan with Jeff Perry and "K.D."

- Do you have enough experience to do a credible job?
- Is there an accessible veterinarian in case your dog becomes sick or is injured?
- How many times each day will you have to perform?
- Will there be a cool quiet place to rest your dog between shows?
- What will your accommodations be?

The answers to those questions, in addition to forming the basis for a future contract, will help you determine whether or not you should take the gig in the first place.

Integral to your canine's safety is the playing surface that you will be performing on. Don't assume that the green grassy playing area you inspect two weeks before your show will be that way when show time arrives. It may

also serve double duty as a horse riding area or a tractor-pull mud hole the day before your show. Have a backup plan and a contractual clause that allows you to move the *situs* of your performance to a safe alternate location.

At many venues, grass may not be an option. At indoor arenas, dirt might be the only available surface. While you may be tempted to think that dirt is an adequate surface for canine disc play, it isn't always. We once engaged in a practice session with our canines on a dirt soccer field in Spain because no grass field could be found. After only five minutes on the dirt surface, we realized that all of our dogs had experienced severe wear on their pads. The innocent looking dirt soccer field contained just enough fine abrasive material (sometimes referred to as decomposed granite or DG) to quickly cause substantial wear to their sensitive pads. If we had practiced a minute or two longer, we might have had to cancel the shows that we had flown across the Atlantic to perform. It is always a good idea to request a sample of any dirt from the organizer before you commit to a show. If the dirt feels gritty or abrasive, then ask for an alternative grassy or carpeted site. If none can be provided, then don't take the booking.

You may also be asked by your host to perform in tight spaces. Many times, we have been asked to perform in small areas in close proximity to spectators. If you are an excellent thrower with a seasoned canine that is *crowd and obstacle aware* then you can probably make things work. If you don't always throw

Peter Bloeme and Jeff Perry during the shooting of "Disc Dog Training DVD."

precisely, or, if your canine is sometimes a bit overly aggressive in its pursuit of the disc, then you should not take such a booking. The last thing in the world you want to do is send your 60-pound bruiser into a crowd at 20 miles per hour. You can expect to hear from lawyers if you make that mistake.

Many *newtons* (see glossary) lose their virginity to Astroturf or carpet at their first paid gig. Not being familiar with the surface they overdo it and practice for five or six minutes. Astroturf is surprisingly abrasive and burned pads can result from overly lengthy or aggressive play on carpet or artificial turf. Keep your sessions short, and do not practice on artificial surfaces out of nervousness. You can easily injure your pet's pads if you overdo it. Also, do not make throws to the margins of the playing area as your dog will be forced to *slam on the brakes* to avoid going into the crowd. This type of abrupt stopping can increase the likelihood of pad damage or other injuries. A good rule of thumb is that it is probably safe to engage in a two-minute performance on artificial turf or carpet, twice per day, for not more than two days. You may be able to go longer, but committing to such shows without knowing how your canine's paws will hold up puts your canine at risk. Always insist on a proper playing surface for your canine. Grass is best, but Astroturf, padded carpet, bare non-abrasive dirt, and other artificial surfaces can be acceptable if you are smart and you regularly check your pet's paws.

CONTRACTS

You may be as good as your word, but not everyone else is. People have short memories and different perspectives

Jeff Perry and "Gilbert" performing for the Dallas Cowboys.

on reality. A written memorialization of your mutual understanding is crucial if you want to minimize aggravation...and get paid! A contract should be written not only to make your arrangement easy to understand, but also impossible to misunderstand. Just as good fences make for good neighbors, good contracts make for good partnerships.

So, what should be in your contract? Anything and everything that you think is material to your ability to perform as requested. Don't leave anything to chance. A few dollars spent wisely with a good attorney will go a long way toward making sure that you and *Bauser* always remain within your comfort zone.

In general, your contract should include clauses that address: 1) the performance surface and location, 2) the number and duration of your shows, 3) your compensation, 4) the items to be supplied or provided by you or the host in con-

junction with your performance(s) such as sound systems, crowd barriers, security, etc., 5) a *force majeure* clause that relieves you of liability for nonperformance if your canine becomes sick or injured, or if, in your sole judgment, the shows cannot be completed safely, 6) your requirements regarding the sale of merchandise (you may want to sell *Team Bauser* hats and T-shirts), 6) language permitting display of sponsor logos, if you have sponsorship, 7) details concerning your liability insurance with the standard being a commercial general liability insurance policy featuring coverage of $1,000,000 per occurrence, with $1,000,000 umbrella coverage, 8) who pays union fees, vendor fees, permit fees, and the like, and 9) miscellaneous details including parking passes, staging areas, etc.

A good attorney will help you create a document that may, in a pinch, prove to be worth its weight in gold.

Peter Bloeme and "Wizard" with Steve Allen, one of the pioneers of late-night television.

PERFORMING
DO'S AND DON'TS

- Do dress and act professionally on and off the field.
- Do obtain liability insurance.
- Do comply with all state, local, and Federal requirements that pertain to how you care for and maintain your performing canines.
- Do make sure that your dog gets a good nature break before you perform to avoid an embarrassing *interruption* in the middle of your performance.
- Do have a back-up plan or substitute performer who can cover for you if your canine is *under the weather* on the show day.
- Don't do anything to give the sport a black eye.
- Don't assume that the person hiring you to do a show will be sophisticated enough to know your needs.
- Don't go soliciting NFL teams for gigs until you have the requisite experience and credentials to represent the sport well. When you are good enough, you will be given opportunities by more experienced competitors who know what works best in the stadium environment.

A FINAL WORD

We remember well our experiences at NFL games, Major League Baseball games and on television shows featuring big-time television personalities like David Letterman, Willard Scott, et al. For the entire day of our gigs, people seemed to know us everywhere we went. We were famous! By the following day, we were anonymous mortals again. The same fate awaits all of you unfortunately. On the other hand, not waking up to the clicking of paparazzi cameras and those *stalker types* is not such a bad thing either! No, sadly, you will never be world famous for your disc dog exploits but, to the community of disc doggers, you can become immortal if you help your brothers and sisters advance in the sport, be kind to animals, rescue dogs from shelters, and always keep the best interests of the sport close to your heart.

Many have achieved this status already and as you progress in the sport you will undoubtedly meet them. In fact, they are household names if your household has disc dogs.

When all is said and done, when the applause fades and its time for the younger folks to take the stage, it will be gratifying for you to look back and know that you have instilled in those who follow, the values and knowledge that will carry the sport to the next level.

GRAVY

Among the most rewarding disc dog demos that I've done over the years, were shows that I did with my dogs "Luke" and "Nick" at St. Jude Children's Research Hospital in Memphis, Tennessee.

For each of the shows, the St. Jude staff would shepherd the young boy and girl patients from their hospital rooms to a small grassy area just outside the hospital. Most of the boys and girls wore little caps signifying a lack of hair attributable to the chemo and radiation therapy that they were receiving. Many also had IV's and those kids rolled their IV carts along beside them just as other kids might carry a backpack on their way to the school bus stop.

At one of the shows, a little girl's mother came down to the performing area to tell me that her daughter was too ill to leave her room but had watched the show from her window. The little girl had insisted that her mom go outside and thank us for doing the show. I asked the girl's mother which window her daughter had watched from, and then I waved to the little girl and did some extra tricks just for her. After the show I gave the mother a trading card with "Luke's" and "Nick's" picture on it and an autographed disc to give to her daughter.

At another St. Jude demo, while waiting on the boys and girls to gather for the show, I glanced toward the lobby of the hospital and saw a little girl about 10 years old sitting in her wheel chair wearing the all-too-familiar cap and with an IV hooked up to her arm. I asked someone to hold the dogs and went inside to say hello.

I knelt down to chat with her and tell her that, in just a few minutes, the dogs were going to do some really neat things just for her. When I finished talking, the little girl looked up at her mother standing close by her side. Her mother repeated my words in sign language to the little girl who, in addition to battling leukemia, was also deaf.

After her mother told her what I had said and what I was going to do, the little girl looked up at me and, with a sweet but frail little voice, said, "thank you."

I left with tears in my eyes but with a happy heart, thankful that because of my dogs "Nick" and "Luke," I had an opportunity to bring joy to her life...if only for a few moments.

— *Bob Evans* Three-Time World Champion with canines "Nick" and "Luke"

Reverse "back vault!"

Peter Bloeme

In writing *Disc Dogs! The Complete Guide* we were reminded many times of the main reason that people become involved in canine disc sports. You can see it on the faces of both human and canine participants. Disc dogging is pure joy!

In many ways, this book is a celebration of the best attributes of those aficionados who participate in canine disc sports. There is, unquestionably, a disc dog family and anyone is welcome to join. Unlike many human sports, the competition between teams is good-natured. People still want to win, of course, but fun is the ultimate goal. A spirit of helpfulness and cooperation will practically knock you over if you are a beginning disc dogger in search of help with your new-found passion. You need only ask, and most competitors will help you as if they have known you for years.

Many folks are intimidated by the idea of competing in front of experienced competitors or large crowds. They needn't be. In all our years of organizing and staging disc dog contests, no team has ever been booed. The

In canine disc sports, it's all about the canine.

Peter Bloeme

Peter Bloeme

Peter Bloeme

Competitions are a great place to mingle with other fun-loving canines.

crowd may laugh along with you as your canine runs to hide in his kennel 15 seconds into your routine…but rest assured, we have all been there and done that at some point in our competitive experiences. Competition is great fun for canines and, for most, the cheering crowd really motivates them to excel.

While it has been 20 years since we competed, we haven't forgotten the thrill of competition and the incredible feeling you get when you are standing on top of that podium, with your best friend, struggling to hoist that championship trophy over your head. Each year, when the Skyhoundz Cup is presented to a new World Champion, those memories come flooding back as if it were only yesterday. Since the time of our respective World Championships we have remained deeply involved in canine disc sports as judges, contest organizers, canine disc manufacturers, canine disc ambassadors, and so on. You could say that we have worn many hats — figuratively and literally! Although the sport has certainly changed over the years, it

has retained its unique charm. It's not about money for most disc doggers because there's little money to be found in the sport. In fact, if you took a poll, you would likely get the impression that monetary prizes might actually be a bad thing for the sport. Disc doggers reason that anything that might cause us to lose focus on the special relationship we have with our canines is to be avoided like the proverbial *load in the road*.

It is impossible to predict how disc dogging will impact your life. However, after all these years we still have people that approach us and tell us that they were motivated to adopt a dog from the pound after hearing us extol the virtues of shelter mutts during a TV interview we gave years earlier. Others relate to us that they became involved in the sport after spectating at one of the many local canine disc competitions that Hyperflite sponsors around the world. Who would have guessed that you can see disc dogs compete in places like Anchorage, Alaska; Billings, Montana; and Liberal, Kansas? Wherever there are dogs, we believe that there can and should be disc dogs. That's why we have made it *job one* to make certain that there are ample opportunities for enthusiasts to have fun with their canines. Hyperflite sponsors more than 150 disc dog competitions as of this writing with more planned for future years.

Through the years we have performed all over the world. We've journeyed to places like Amsterdam, Barcelona, Berlin, Brussels, Budapest, Mexico City, Milan, Prince Edward Island, Seoul, Shanghai, and Tokyo. We could write another book and fill it with the memories from each of the many shows and clinics that we have staged in those exotic places.

On many of our early trips, very few dog owners, if any, had even heard of canine disc sports. During each of those trips we took the time to *sow seeds.* We gave clinics, talked to dog owners, helped people learn to throw, and freely shared our knowledge with enthusiasts. We encouraged them to give the sport a try. Our philosophy…plant enough seeds and, eventually, something will grow. Looking back, we wouldn't have predicted that the sport would gain a foothold in China, Estonia, Hungary, Poland, or Russia. But, at Hyperflite, disc orders come in every day from enthusiasts in the most unlikely places.

While we can't predict the future, we know that canine disc sports will continue to be popular with those who want to live life to the fullest and involve their canine companions in the fun. Your journey is just beginning and you and your best friend will surely have the times of your lives. After all, disc dogging is love at first bite!

Semper Fido!

— **Peter Bloeme and Jeff Perry**

Jeff Perry judging at the 2006 Hyperflite Skyhoundz World Canine Disc Championship.

Skyhoundz World Championship Cup.

Disc Dog Glossary
Chapter 15

Airbounce — An airbounce is made by forcing the bottom of a rapidly-spinning disc toward the ground as it is thrown toward its intended target. A cushion of air builds up under the disc preventing it from impacting the ground, while the forward motion of the disc generates lift that causes the disc to rise back into the air after its close encounter with terra firma. A variety of deliveries are possible.

Airbrush — A throw made by striking or *brushing* the rim of a spinning disc with a hand or foot to alter its flight path.

Ambijumpsterous — The demonstrated ability of certain canines to perform *backflips* in either direction.

Anhyzer — A throwing technique that causes a disc to arc, or rotate, in the direction that it is spinning. The opposite of hyzer.

Ashley Whippet — The best-known disc dog in the world made famous by the exploits of the deviously daring Alex Stein.

AWI — Ashley Whippet Invitational.

Back Vault — A trick in which a canine employs a thrower's back as a launching pad from which to attain greater height or distance while catching a disc.

Backflip — A twisting (usually) jumping catch made by a canine of a disc tossed vertically (usually) over the dog's head. The throw causes its body to flip backwards while the canine's momentum causes the canine's body to continue in an arc that approximates the path of the thrown disc. The canine then lands facing the thrower. Any number of variations is possible. The opposite of a *frontflip*.

Sven Van Driessche

Backhand Throw — The standard throw in canine disc sports used in Distance/Accuracy events and any time long throws are required.

BC — Border Collie

Big Gun — An accomplished long distance thrower.

Bossy (also Baussie) — A Border Collie/Australian Shephard Mix.

Bottomed Out — A landing made by a canine that results in impact of the canine body with the ground.

Butterfly — A throw made by causing a disc to tumble, end-over-end, toward the jaws of a waiting canine.

Butterlips — A dog that grabs then instantly drops the disc.

Can-Am Games — A Canadian-American collaborative disc dog contest that brings together canines from several Canadian provinces and many American states.

Catapult — The name first given to the trick now known more popularly as the *leg* or *thigh vault*.

Chest Vault — A *vaulting* trick that requires that a canine push off of the chest of the thrower before making a catch. Many variations are possible.

Clay Pigeon — A disc made with inferior plastic that shatters in cold weather.

Crash — An uncoordinated landing, usually not on all four paws or a collision between thrower and canine.

Custered — Having your disc dog routine interrupted by a wayward spectator or canine. E.G. *I got Custered by that dog;* or *did you see that guy Custer me?*

GRAVY

In the summer of 2006, while I was still fairly new to canine disc sports, I experienced the type of challenge that I wouldn't wish on anyone. The trouble started when I, inexplicably, kept getting sick. Then one day, my knee swelled up so bad that I went to the hospital to have it looked at. I was informed that, due to a previous injury, I had developed a life-threatening infection in my knee. My doctor informed me that there was a 50/50 chance I could die. I remember lying in the hospital bed late one night truly feeling at that point that I might not make it. I started to pray and I promised God that if he would let me hug my wife one more time, visit the University of Notre Dame one more time (I'm a big Irish football fan), and let me throw one more disc to each of my dogs — then I would be ready to go. Well, with lots of prayer and some serious rehabilitation, I finally recovered.

That fall I knew I wasn't ready to compete again but I gave it a shot anyway. I was truly an emotional wreck and overcome with joy just looking down at my dogs "Rocket" and "Gipper" and realizing that, after such a close call, here I was, able to go out and compete again. As I recall, we did OK — but I could have cared less about our scores as long as I could play with my buddies again.

This injury gave me such a different perspective on life and the sport of disc dogging. I no longer go out there with the desire to win first. Instead, when I compete, I do so with the philosophy of just having fun with my dogs, enjoying my time with them, and making people smile.

If we finish in the top tier, then that makes the true reward just a little sweeter.

— Mark Muir, Hyperflite Skyhoundz Open Division World Finalist

Dawg — The southern version of dog.

Disc — The circular wing-shaped platter that makes disc dog sports possible.

DiscDogathon — Hyperflite sponsored events that feature Boomerang, Bullseye, Distance/Accuracy, Extreme Distance, Freestyle, Spot Landing, Time Trial, and Club Choice events.

Disc Drive — Unabashed, crazed passion for the disc.

Disctionary — This Glossary.

Distance/Accuracy (D/A) — A Skyhoundz short distance event with scoring zones that begin to diminish in size the farther they are removed from the throwing line.

DNF — Did not finish. Usually, a canine that is withdrawn from competition because of injury or a scheduling conflict.

Dog-eh — Canadian for dog.

Doowug — What they call dogs in New York City.

Face Skid — What can happen when your dog tries to catch a worm burner.

FDDO — Flying Disc Dog Open. A contest series featuring canine freestyle, distance, speed disc, and obstacle course events.

Fetch and Catch — A general description of a catch and return event, employing one disc, not involving freestyle.

Fetching — A description that always applies to female disc doggers.

Fidelis Caninus Amiculus — An inscription found on Hyperflite Award Medals that means faithful canine friend.

Flabrador — An overweight Labrador Retriever.

Fly By — When a dog jumps for a disc and completely misses it.

Freestyle — A choreographed routine involving a dog and human team that perform trick sequences for an allotted time with an allotted amount of discs.

Frisbee — A trademarked term for a brand of flying discs that is used in canine disc competition.

Handler — The term handler, used by some disc doggers, implies that we *hu-*

Competitors posing for Hyperflite's upcoming, "Women of Disc Dogs" calendar.

Jeff Perry

Jeff Perry

Once the competition begins, the competitors get a lot less friendly...

mans are the boss and that dogs merely do our bidding. However, one could argue that our dogs may be more deserving of the *handler* title than we humans since they frequently *handle* our bad throws without any help from us whatsoever! We prefer a term like *trainer* because that better describes our true role. In the context of competition, *teammate* best describes the interaction between canine and human.

Hyperflite — A trademarked term for a brand of flying discs that is used in canine disc competitions.

Hyzer — The angle placed on a disc that helps counteract lost stability as a disc slows down.

IDDHA — International Disc Dog Handlers' Association.

Jawtograph —The bite signature left on a disc by a toothy canine.

Juggling — A trick in which two discs are tossed repeatedly to a canine so that it appears as if they are being juggled between thrower and canine.

Lame — A *cheesy* trick sequence or an injury to a canine paw, leg, or shoulder resulting in an obvious limp.

Lander, Irv —The man who established the first disc dog series and provided fatherly guidance to all of the energetic and idealistic *kids* that helped make canine disc sports what they are today. Many of these *kids* now stage their own disc dog competition series.

Leg Vault — A *vaulting* trick that begins with a canine pushing off of the thigh of the thrower immediately prior to catching the disc.

McIntire, Eldon — An influential early disc dogger who, along with Alex Stein,

Apparently you can teach an "old dog" new tricks. Evans is a three-time World Canine Disc Champion with "Luke" and "Nick."

helped boost the popularity of disc dog sports at their genesis.

MicroDog — A smaller canine as defined by Skyhoundz rules that competes in the MicroDog division of the Hyperflite Skyhoundz World Canine Disc Championship.

Mini-Distance — A short distance event with no side boundaries.

Multiples — A series of rapidly thrown throws designed to demonstrate a canine's catching and dropping capability.

Mutt — The perfect dog for canine disc sports.

Nail Delay — A human freestyle trick in which a spinning disc is balanced on the finger tip of a thrower who then delivers the disc to a waiting canine in some fashion or another.

Newton (also Noob, Newt, Newbie, Newdist) — A non-derisive reference to a disc-dog rookie.

Old Yeller — A term used to describe a competitor that enthusiastically yells at his or her canine during competition.

Over — A trick in which the canine leaps over some portion of the human teammate.

Overhand Wrist-Flip — A trick throw considerably easier to demonstrate than to describe. Perfecting this throw is challenging for many disc doggers.

Pairs Freestyle — Freestyle routines performed by two throwers and one canine. This event was first included in the Hyperflite Skyhoundz World Canine Disc Championship, as a demonstration event, in 2003. The first Pairs Freestyle World Championship title was awarded in 2005.

Pawtograph — A stamped canine *paw signature*.

Porcupine — A severely damaged disc that is in need of retirement.

It's no wonder that Border Collies are known for "The Eye."

Prey Drive — Although the term is popular with some trainers, few would argue that a disc dog's motivation for chasing a disc is tied to some prehistoric instinct to catch and kill prey. Dogs love to play and have fun just like we humans do. We prefer the term *disc drive* to describe a canine's desire to catch a disc and thereby win our praise.

Pyur Jur — What disc dogging represents to all of us (See *Disc Dog Training DVD* — Bloopers Section).

Quadruped — A long distance canine catching competition.

Rebarks — The name given to the canine booties worn by disc dogs that perform indoors on hard surfaces such as basketball courts.

Rescue — A canine rescued from a shelter or rescue organization. Also, the point in a flubbed disc dog routine when a timekeeper, mercifully, yells *time!*

Roller — A throw that causes a disc to spin rapidly and roll on its edge until grabbed by a canine.

Sailboat — A disc thrown into a crosswind — with improper technique — that tacks its way (à la sailboat) off of the playing field and into the next county.

Sandbagger — A competitor who deliberately understates his or her canine disc abilities in order to enter a competitive class from which he or she can pirate trophies from less-experienced novice disc doggers. Hunting sandbaggers is legal in all 50 states, Europe, and Asia and there is no limit to the number of sandbaggers that may be taken during the season which runs from January 1-December 31.

Sidearm Throw — The predominant throw used in the sport of Ultimate. The sidearm throw is used in canine disc sports by many competitors though it is slightly more difficult to control. The disc also spins rapidly in the opposite direction of the backhand throw which can make it more challenging for a canine to catch.

Skip — A skip occurs when a thrower causes the outside edge of a thrown disc to strike the ground and then return to normal flight.

Skyhoundz —The largest disc dog series in the world, featuring more than 100 local competitions in the U.S. as well as regional, open and international qualifiers leading to the Hyperflite Skyhoundz World Canine Disc Championship.

Spin — The rotation of a disc about its central axis. Spin imparts stability to a disc in flight. Also, any trick in which a canine turns rapidly about its central axis during a disc dog routine.

Spinner — A variant of the butterfly in which the disc moves laterally (like a thrown football) rather than vertically.

Spit — Another way of saying *Drop*.

Stall — A component of a canine trick sequence in which a canine momentarily pauses or *stalls*, usually on the back or feet of a trainer, before making a catch or dismounting to continue a freestyle routine.

Stein, Alex —The human catalyst for disc dog sports whose exploits first introduced America to disc-catching canines.

Super Star —What all of our dogs represent to us.

Taco — What happens when a dentally-obsessive canine folds a disc in-half while the disc is in the canine's mouth.

Take — A trick in which a canine is commanded to take a disc from the thrower's hand, body, mouth, etc.

Tap — A trick in which a canine uses its nose to *tap* a thrown disc back to a thrower instead of catching it. It is usually done several times in a row for emphasis. This challenging trick will bring the house down if done well.

Tip —A freestyle move that occurs when a human uses a finger, fist, elbow, foot, or other body part to bounce a spinning disc back into the air, often repeatedly.

Throwing a Donut — Getting a zero in Distance/Accuracy.

Throwing a Rope —A hard level throw with little fluctuation in altitude from the thrower's release, to the canine's catch.

Thumb Throw — The thumb throw, or thumber as it is sometimes called, is a rapidly spinning throw usually made with a side-armed delivery. The disc is typically gripped between the thumb and the index finger, hence the name. A number of variations are possible.

Two-Handed Push Toss — A short distance throw in which both hands are used to impart spin and momentum to a disc. Push tosses may be made either vertically or horizontally.

UFO —A canine contest series featuring freestyle, throw and catch, and longshot.

Upside-Down Throw — An inverted throw made with a variety of deliveries.

USDDN — U.S. Disc Dog Nationals. A canine contest series featuring freestyle and toss and fetch rounds.

Vaulting Vest — A neoprene rubber diving vest used to protect a human thrower from the claws of a canine when said canine uses the thrower's chest or back as a launching pad.

Wind Dummy — The first person to compete on a windy day, or everyone that competes before you on a windy day if you have a good round.

World Champion — A team that has managed to overcome numerous challenges and win top honors, at a Hyperflite Skyhoundz World Canine Disc Championship, in one of four Skyhoundz divisions including Open, Sport, MicroDog, and Pairs Freestyle.

Worm Burner — A disc thrown too low and too fast for a canine to catch.

XDC — An acronym for Hyperflite's Xtreme Distance Challenge, a contest for teams that appreciate ultra-long distance throws.

Frank Buckland attempts to hypnotize the judges.

Jeff Hoot

Disc Dog Commands

Chapter 16

Because of the explosive growth of canine disc sports around the world, we felt that it would be prudent to include the basic disc dog commands in a variety of languages for your enjoyment.

We can't vouch for the unfailing accuracy of the words shown, but they have been provided by disc dog enthusiasts in the various listed countries. The commands are spelled phonetically in English to aid in pronunciation.

Also, many international trainers may choose to use English commands rather than the commands of their native language. So, when you say *suware* to a Japanese dog he may just look at you funny and wonder why you don't speak English!

The commands we have chosen for translation are: *Catch, Come, Down, Drop, Go, Jump, Sit, Spin, Stay, and Wait.*

Enjoy!

English	Chinese	Croatian
Catch	Jie Zhu	Uhvatiti
Come	Lai	Dodi
Down	Pah Shia	Lezi
Drop	Fong Shia	Kap
Go	Zou	Ici
Jump	Tiao	Skok
Sit	Zuo	Sjedi
Spin	Zhuan	Vrtnja
Stay	Ting Liu	Cekaj
Wait	Deng	Oklijevati
	Czech	**Danish**
Catch	Drz	Hugge
Come	Ke mne	Her
Down	Lehni	Daek
Drop	Pust	Tabe
Go	Vpred	Ga
Jump	Hop	Hoppe
Sit	Sedni	Sit
Spin	Prist	Rotere
Stay	Zustan	Bliv
Wait	Stuj	Vent
	Dutch	**Estonian**
Catch	Vang	Puuk
Come	Hier	Siia
Down	Af	Lama
Drop	Los	Piisk
Go	Vooruit	Kaik
Jump	Spring	Hupe
Sit	Zit	Istu
Spin	Rond	Keerd
Stay	Blijf	Seisa
Wait	Wacht	Ootamine

English	Finnish	French
Catch	Pure	Mord
Come	Tnne	Ici
Down	Maahan	Coucher
Drop	Irti	Donne
Go	Eteen	En avant
Jump	Yli	Saute
Sit	Istu	Assis
Spin	Kehrata	Tourne
Stay	Paikka	Reste
Wait	Seiso	Attend

	German	Hebrew
Catch	Fang	T'fos
Come	Komm / Hier	Bo
Down	Platz	Artzah
Drop	Aus	A'zov
Go	Los	Lech
Jump	Spring	Ke'fotz
Sit	Sitz	Shev
Spin	Dreh	Tsovev
Stay	Bleib	He'sha'er
Wait	Warte	Chakeh

	Hungarian	Italian
Catch	Fogd	Morde
Come	Gyere	Vieni
Down	Feküdj	Terra
Drop	Ereszd	Dare
Go	Menj	Davanti
Jump	Ugorj	Salto
Sit	Ülj	Seduto
Spin	Forogj	Gira
Stay	Maradj	Resta
Wait	Várj	Aspetta

Sven Van Driessche

	Japanese	**Korean**
Catch	Tore	Mul-uh
Come	Koi	E-ri-wa
Down	Fuse	Up-du-ryo
Drop	Dase	Noah
Go	Ike	Ga
Jump	Tobe	Tui-uh
Sit	Suware	An-ja
Spin	Maware	Dol-ah
Stay	Mate	Mum-chua
Wait	Mate	Gi-da-ryo
	Polish	**Portugese**
Catch	Łap	Pega
Come	Do Mnie	Junto / Vem
Down	Waruj or Leż	Deita
Drop	Puść	Solta
Go	Go	Vá
Jump	Hop	Pula
Sit	Siad	Senta
Spin	Obrót	Gira
Stay	Zostań	Fica
Wait	Czekaj	Para

	Russian	Spanish
Catch	Lovi'	Aqui
Come	Ko-mne'	Ven Aqui
Down	Lezha't	Echate
Drop	Bro's	Gota
Go	Idi'	Vaya
Jump	Pri'gai	Salto
Sit	Side't	Sientate
Spin	Vrashcha'y	Vuelta
Stay	Stoya't	Quiento
Wait	Zhdi'	Espera

Sven Van Driessche

Walking on air to catch a "Jawz disc."

Sven Van Driessche

As we reviewed thousands of photos for *Disc Dogs! The Complete Guide*, we came across quite a few that begged for clever captions. We decided to include them here and let you do your own wordsmithing.

Sven Van Driessche

Thom Gillott

Sven Van Driessche

Sven Van Driessche

Sven Van Driessche

Sven Van Driessche

Sven Van Driessche

Peter Bloeme

Sven Van Driessche

Sven Van Driessche

Jay Moldow

Jeff Perry

Sven Van Driessche

Sven Van Driessche

Sven Van Driessche

Sven Van Driessche

Angie Stanaway

Sven Van Driessche

Sven Van Driessche

Jay Moldow

Sven Van Driessche

Sven Van Driessche

Sven Van Driessche

Peter Bloeme

Sven Van Driessche

Sven Van Driessche

Sven Van Driessche

Thom Gillott

Peter Bloeme

Sven Van Driessche

Lynn Hoot

Sven Van Driessche

Sven Van Driessche

Sven Van Driessche

Sven Van Driessche

Sven Van Driessche

Sven Van Driessche

Jay Moldow

Sven Van Driessche

Jeff Hoot

Peter Bloeme

Sven Van Driessche

Sven Van Driessche

Jeff Hoot

Sven Van Driessche

Sven Van Driessche

Sven Van Driessche

Sven Van Driessche

Thom Gillott

Sven Van Driessche

Sven Van Driessche

Jay Moldow

Sven Van Driessche

Sven Van Driessche

Sven Van Driessche

Jeff Hoot

Statue of "Beelzebowser," a mythical prehistoric disc dog.

Peter Bloeme

Up, up and away!

About the Authors

PETER BLOEME

Hyperflite co-founder, Peter Bloeme is director of the Skyhoundz Championships. In this role, he manages more than 100 Local Championships, 10 U.S. and International Qualifiers, and the World Championship.

Bloeme's career of tossing, skipping, bouncing, spinning, and twirling a plastic disc began when he finished third overall and first in distance at the Junior National Frisbee Championships at the age of 15. In 1976, at the age of 19, he won the World Frisbee Championships at the Rose Bowl in California before 40,000 disc fans.

In 1983, Bloeme added a new element to his flying disc repertoire — a black and white Border Collie named *Whirlin'Wizard*. The two went on to win the 1984 World Canine Disc Championships making *Wizard*, at less than 2 years old, the youngest dog, at the time, to win the title. At the same time, Bloeme became the only person to win a world title both by himself and with his dog.

In 1990, Bloeme added a little magic to his routine — literally — with the addition of *Magic*, a black and white Australian Shepherd. Over the years, Bloeme, *Wizard*, and *Magic* performed hundreds of disc dog demonstrations at sporting events including Major League Baseball, National Basketball Association, National Football League, and World Football League games.

Bloeme and his canine companions have also performed numerous times before sold-out stadium crowds all around the world. They have performed half-time shows at sporting events and have made public appearances in countries including Belgium, Canada, China, England, France, Germany, Hungry, Italy, Japan, Mexico, Puerto Rico, Spain, Sweden, and The Netherlands. Perhaps his

Peter Bloeme has "Wizard" jump over him in NYC.

most notable appearance was at the 1995 Japanese Baseball All-Star Game in Hiroshima, Japan where, after the seventh inning, the game was stopped for a ten-minute exhibition by Bloeme and four Japanese dogs. Bloeme's performance was viewed live by a sold-out crowd of 40,000 fans plus an estimated 26 million people on television via the Tokyo Broadcasting System.

During the 1970's, Bloeme served as technical advisor to CBS Sports for a half-hour television special on Frisbee and toured Europe as a representative of the International Frisbee Association.

Bloeme and his dogs have appeared on television in the U.S. hundreds of times, including featured appearances on shows such as *Good Morning America, Late Night with David Letterman,* and on CNN and ESPN. You may remember seeing *Wizard* opening the Disney movie, *Flight of the Navigator.* In a Miller Lite television ad, Bloeme was responsible for the on-camera disc action. *Wizard* even had a walk-on role in the spot. Bloeme has also served twice as the color commentator for Animal Planet in their one-hour specials on the World Championships.

In 2001, Bloeme, Jeff Perry (1989 World Champion and Hall of Famer), and Greg Perry founded Hyperflite, a company dedicated to developing advanced disc technology. Their first disc, the *K-10* for dogs was introduced in July of 2001.

Bloeme is author of the book, *Frisbee Dogs: How to Raise, Train and Compete,* a 192-page paperback, illustrated with over 300 photographs and the book, *Skyhoundz Images,* an 80-page hardcover photo book on the sport with captions in English, Japanese and Spanish ($19.95 U.S.).

Bloeme also co-produced, along with Jeff Perry, the internationally-acclaimed *Disc Dog Training DVD,* the top-selling disc dog training DVD of all time.

JEFF PERRY

Hyperflite co-founder Jeff Perry and his mixed-breed, animal shelter adoptee, *Gilbert* won the 1989 World Canine Disc Championship in Dallas, Texas. Prior to taking the World title, Perry and *Gilbert* won the Southeast Regional Championship for three consecutive years. *Gilbert* and Perry went on to be featured on NBC's top-rated *Today Show,* along with numerous appearances on CNN, ESPN, and other national and international media over the years. As a member of the ALPO Canine Disc Celebrity Touring Team, Perry was a media spokesperson for the 10-year period in which ALPO sponsored the Canine disc Championships.

In countless interviews and public appearances, Perry has consistently extolled the virtues of adopting shelter animals. According to Perry, shelter mutts make wonderful companions and great disc dogs.

Perry and his canines have performed hundreds of times before sold-out stadium crowds at professional football and baseball games and at other events held all over the world. Internationally, Perry has performed before huge crowds at Olympic Stadiums in Berlin and Barcelona and has made public appearances in Belgium, Canada, China, Spain, Germany, Hungary, Italy, Japan, Mexico, and Puerto Rico. *Gilbert* and Perry were featured entertainers at the prestigious *Colare de Oro,* the Italian equivalent of the Westminster dog show.

While performing in Japan, Perry met the Crown Prince and Princess of Japan (the future emperor and empress of Japan) after one of more than 200 shows that he performed over a four-month period at the *Animal Kingdom* in Nasu. While in Japan, Perry and his dog *Cosmic K.D.* also entertained thousands of spectators in the Tokyo Dome.

After retiring from competition in 1989, Perry served as the Chief Judge of the World Canine Disc Championship for 15 years.

Perry co-founded Hyperflite in 2000 and, shortly thereafter, designed and patented the revolutionary *K-10 disc*, the first canine disc designed exclusively for canine competition.

Perry co-produced the internationally-acclaimed *Disc Dog Training DVD*, the top-selling disc dog training DVD of all time.

Perry also serves as a Contributing Editor for *Flying Disc Magazine*.

A strong proponent of the health and fitness benefits of canine disc play for dogs and owners, Perry founded one of the first canine disc dog clubs in the country. Over the years, Perry has taught countless canine-disc aficionados to throw flying discs and helped even elite-level competitors improve their throwing abilities.

In addition to his canine disc activities, Perry still finds time to engage in some of his other favorite pursuits — climbing, backpacking and flying. Perry, a skilled pilot, has flown powered aircraft and hang gliders for more than 25 years and has logged more than 2,000 hours in many types of aircraft. In fact, his aeronautical experience and understanding of aeronautical principles were instrumental in the design of the Hyperflite *K-10 disc*.

Perry received a Bachelor of Science degree (B.S.) in Journalism from the University of Maryland, a Juris Doctor degree (J.D.) from Mercer University and a Master of Laws in International Law (LL.M.) from the University of Miami.

Jeff Perry's "Gilbert" was known for his mastery of "backflips."

Peter Bloeme

Follow the leader — Danny Eggleston and Christina Curtis with "Guinan."

Disc Dogs! Index

Sven Van Driessche

Every canine breed, with the exception of the Chow, has a pink tongue. Chow tongues are jet black. If your mixed-breed canine has black on its tongue, then there is almost certainly a Chow in your mutt's ancestry.

Long Photography, Inc.

Peter Biloerie

A nice reverse overhand wrist-flip throw.

A Final Word of Thanks...

In the past eight years, we have received many emails, notes, and letters of thanks from Hyperflite's customers. We always appreciate these words of encouragement, but, we are mindful that the accolades more properly belong to all those who make the world a better place for their canine friends.

With great appreciation, we reprint one such letter, along with accompanying photographs, for your enjoyment.   — **Peter Bloeme, Greg Perry, and Jeff Perry**

We love your "Jawz discs!" There is no better disc on the market!

My 9-year-old Blue Heeler, "Little Bear'" is blind from degenerative retina disorder and never leaves home without his "Jawz disc!" His "Jawz" is like an enabler for his herding instinct and he controls whatever situation he is in with his "Jawz" clenched firmly between his teeth! Even when I am backcountry snowboarding in Valdez, Alaska, "Little Bear" always brings his "Jawz" along for the ride!

"Little Bear's" hearing is extremely sharp and it is hard to tell that he cannot see, so he is very persistent in finding the back of your leg with his "Jawz." As soon as he bumps it up against you, that means it's time for another throw! He also loves to drag his "Jawz" all around the snow, sand, or anything soft he can scoot it across! He often creates interesting designs and circles in the snow! Sometimes, when I throw his "Jawz" into the wind, it hovers just right, and "Little Bear," blind and all, still manages to snatch his "Jawz" out of the air! When that happens, you can tell it makes him proud even though I know he probably longs for days long gone when he could still see.

Since we discovered your "Jawz discs" a number of years ago, it has remained his very favorite disc ever!

We are down to one new, one pretty good, and one very-worn "Jawz disc," but, after several years, he has yet to shred a single one. Well, its finally time to restock because a "thief dog" recently stole one of his favorites.

— **Dan Hawksworth** and *Little Bear*

Disc Dogs! The Complete Guide Reviews

If disc dogging were a university course then "Disc Dogs!" would be the textbook. From initiation to graduation this book has something for everyone. Even advanced teams will find new tricks and useful tips to improve their throws and consistency. I had to run out and try a few! I particularly enjoyed the stories and photos of teams past and present. They helped to add insight into how the sport has evolved.
— **Dennis Alexander, Four-Time Skyhoundz World Finalist**

Four years ago, we were invited by a long-time disc dogger to watch a Skyhoundz Local Championship and we've been hooked ever since. When we first got started, the only way to learn was to attend competitions and pick the brains of other competitors. If only "Disc Dogs! The Complete Guide" was available when we were starting out.

This light-hearted read is easy to follow with numerous step-by-step photos that could teach even the most stubborn dog new tricks!

For potential competitors, "Disc Dogs!" has all the information needed including rules, field layouts, and tips for bringing your best performance to the field.
— **John and Shannon Bilheimer, Skyhoundz World Champions**

I found "Disc Dogs! The Complete Guide" to be "E²," both educational and entertaining. I particularly enjoyed the history section and the endearing "Gravy" stories that only served to confirm what I already new — that disc doggers are the salt of the earth.

In fewer and sweeter words, the book was "pure joy!"
— **Frank Montgomery, Three-Time Skyhoundz World Finalist**

Bloeme and Perry have outdone themselves. "Disc Dogs! The Complete Guide" was a fantastic read from cover-to-cover. It provides great information for the newbie. It also serves as a review for the seasoned veteran. More importantly it is a reminder of how blessed we are to be on the field with our special canines. "Disc Dogs!" captures the fun and camaraderie of our sport. — **Theresa Musi, Three-Time Skyhoundz World Finalist**

Finally, a step-by-step guide for anyone who wants to become involved in the sport of disc-dogging! This well-planned book is helpful not only to newbies, but also seasoned competitors. It is fun, well illustrated, and has great action shots demonstrating both throws and team movements. I would highly recommend "Disc Dogs! The Complete Guide" to anyone wanting to become involved in canine disc sports. You can bet it will become a staple for our disc dog club members and friends! Thanks, Peter and Jeff, for finally creating this much needed resource!
— **Tracy Custer, Five-Time Skyhoundz World Finalist**

This book is a must for any disc dogger!!! — **Nyle "Swanee" Swainston, Gig Harbor, WA**

This phenomenal treatise is unequaled in the world of canine sports. The information provided gives every enthusiast precisely what is needed for success in the park or on the playing field. — **David Turrentine, Atlanta, GA**

Disc Dogs! Reviews (Continued)

Bloeme and Perry bring an amazing amount of experience to this project. They've done it all, with a combined total of more than 50 years of experience including both human and canine disc sports. In that time, they have travelled throughout the world, competing, teaching, and promoting canine disc sports. "Disc Dogs! The Complete Guide" is a must for anyone interested in the sport, from those just starting out to those who are preparing for championship play.
— Dan "Stork" Roddick, PhD
Former Director of the International Frisbee Association (IFA)
Former President of the World Flying Disc Federation (WFDF)
Charter Member Frisbee, Ultimate and Disc Golf Halls of Fame

Whether you're a seasoned competitor or just beginning your own fascinating journey in disc dog sports, you will enjoy and benefit from the information you find in these pages. If this book had been available when I started tossing plastic to my dogs, it would not have taken eight years to qualify for my first World Championship and it may not have taken another nine years after that to finally win a World Championship!
— Chuck Middleton, 2002 Skyhoundz World Canine Disc Champion,
Open and Sport Divisions, Skyhoundz Lifetime Achievement Award Recipient

The first time the book touched my hands there was no reading involved, it was front-to-back just enjoying the images alone. High speed action photography is not a simple matter, yet this book is loaded with a very nice collection of images. Couple that with the authors' talent for communicating their experience and knowledge and you end up with a disc dog book that is in a league all by itself. It's another standing ovation for Peter Bloeme and Jeff Perry.
— Jeff Hoot, Director, The Quadruped

The structure and thoroughness of the book are without equal, but I would buy "Disc Dogs!" for the photos alone.
— Paul West, Four-Time Skyhoundz World Finalist

Finally! A comprehensive book about canine disc sports. "Disc Dogs! The Complete Guide" is jam-packed with information for the canine disc enthusiast. If only this book had been available when I started out in the sport. It answers many of the questions I had as a novice. Even now as an experienced competitor, I found the chapter on competition, with its gems of wisdom about disc management, music selection, and throwing in the wind, particularly helpful. This book is a "must have" for anyone starting out in the sport of canine disc, and a good reference book for any disc dogger's library.
— Jackie Parkin, Two-Time Skyhoundz World Finalist

Peter Bloeme and Jeff Perry are the Babe Ruth and Mickey Mantle of disc dogging. This "must have" book will become the bible for anyone involved in our sport.
— George Freeman, Mount Vernon, WA

"Disc Dogs!" is a must-have for every disc dog aficionado! A job well done is an understatement.
— Sven Van Driessche, Edegem, The Netherlands